*Studies in Educational Theory*
*of the John Dewey Society*        **NUMBER 3**

*Whitehead on Education*

# *Whitehead on Education*

## by HAROLD B. DUNKEL

OHIO STATE UNIVERSITY PRESS

# Foreword

IN VIEW OF the fact that Alfred North Whitehead is one of the most original and imaginative of twentieth-century philosophers, his views on education are of special interest. Both his general philosophy and his writings on education are provocative, full of suggestions for action, and fresh. As one who was "alive with living thoughts," he wore his vast erudition with imagination; and both in his classes and in his writings he fulfilled admirably what he took to be the double function of the teacher: (1) that of eliciting "enthusiasm by resonance from his own personality," and (2) that of creating "the environment of a larger knowledge and firmer purpose."

Whitehead was wonderfully able to convey a sense of significance, or what he called "the sense of importance." If, on the one hand, he held that we learn by doing, on the other, he maintained that education consists in "the habitual vision of greatness." His sensitivity, urbanity, insight, eagerness to free us from "inert ideas," wisdom, and moral earnestness shine through his writings.

In a series sponsored by the John Dewey Society it is perhaps appropriate to note Dewey's apt statement concerning Whitehead in his essay on "The Philosophy of Whitehead" (in P. A. Schilpp, *The Philosophy of Alfred North Whitehead* [2nd ed.; New York: Tudor Publishing Company, 1951], 659) : "He has opened an immensely fruitful new path for subsequent philosophy to follow. . . . The result is an almost incomparable suggestiveness on all sorts of topics—in case a mind is not closed to suggestion from a new source."

Coming from a family of clergymen and schoolmasters, his experiences at Cambridge University, the University of London, and Harvard University—as a student, professor, dean, chairman of administrative academic councils, supervisor of London education, and member of innumerable committees concerned with various phases and levels of education—his lively interest in the universities of this country, and his concern with the problems of higher education in a modern industrial civilization gave him an unusual background for studies in comparative education. In addition, as the following passage from *The Aims of Education* shows, he was deeply convinced of the crucial significance of education:

> When one considers in its length and in its breadth the importance of this question of the education of a nation's young, the broken lives, the defeated hopes, the national failures, which result from the frivolous inertia with which it is treated, it is difficult to restrain within oneself a savage rage. In the conditions of modern life the rule is absolute, the race which does not value trained intelligence is doomed.

He felt that the novel adaptation of education being worked out at the University of London and at various schools in this country was one of the factors which might save civilization and that it performed a task analagous to the monasteries a thousand years earlier.

In spite of his zest for education and his numerous essays with educational significance, there are, however, at least three major difficulties for one who would relate Whitehead's philosophy of education to his general philosophy; and these difficulties hinder effective use of his suggestions for education. In the first place, to our great regret, there is no book of his which expounds his general philosophy in its bearing on educational issues and problems as, say, Dewey's *Democracy and Education* did for his views.

In the second place, there is no single simple exposition of his cosmology and general philosophy which provides all the relevant background material for his ideas on education. *Process and Reality,* which has more for this purpose than any other single volume, is far from simple, and it needs to be supplemented by material drawn from his other writings. Neither *Science and the Modern World* nor *Adventures of Ideas* provides as much; and *Modes of Thought,* which offers perhaps the least technical of Whitehead's own expositions of his general approach, needs even more supplementation than either of these volumes. The available summaries of his views, moreover, are pointed more toward metaphysics, theory of knowledge, or philosophy of science than toward education.

Perhaps the greatest difficulty for non-philosophy students, however, is Whitehead's formidable technical vocabulary. It may be more than a coincidence that one who at one time knew by heart parts of the *Critique of Pure Reason* should make use in his own philosophy of the largest number of new technical terms in any major system since Kant's. But Whitehead was trying to say something new, something not yet crystallized into conventional modes of expression, and he apparently felt that there were less serious risks in creating new terms than in relying exclusively upon using the old ones to mean something different. The old ones, to be sure, will require some restatement, too, in the new system. At any rate, he was convinced that "no language can be anything but elliptical, requiring a leap of the imagination to understand its meaning in its relevance to immediate experience," that we must "start from verbal expressions which, when taken by themselves with the current meanings of their words, are ill-defined and ambiguous," and that we then work to clarify meanings and define terms more sharply.

It is Professor Dunkel's great merit in the present volume that he has done much to overcome or minimize these three major difficulties for students who would relate Whitehead's philosophy of education to his general philosophy. *Whitehead on Education* provides an exposition of his general philosophy and cosmology in their bearing on educational issues and problems. Professor Dunkel helps us see that Whitehead's views on education represent not simply scattered insights and comments but rather a coherent whole with significant suggestions for our educational problems.

He has performed a double service for us in connection with Whitehead's vocabulary. In the first place, he has helped clarify the technical terms; and secondly and more importantly, he has explained the reasons for this formidable terminology as a necessary consequence of Whitehead's attempt to offer a new conceptual framework in terms of which we may observe and analyze experience.

In terms of Professor Dunkel's exposition, Whitehead's aims and principles acquire greater clarity and relevance; and if *the aim* of education for Whitehead is, as Professor Dunkel suggests, "to enable the human organism to effect, through adventure, that sort of self-creation which will be a good patterning of the data available in that epoch and which will constitute a creative advance into novelty," who among us can fail to be excited by the prospect of following out the implications for curriculums, students, and teachers? There are some who charge that Whitehead expects too much either as interpreted above or as holding that the ideal for every pupil should be knowing something well and doing something well; but though there may be varying degrees of achievement, a lower aim almost certainly underestimates human potentialities, and we may be happy that Whitehead sets his sights high.

Perhaps Professor Dunkel's greatest contribution, however, consists in the fact that because of his monograph many of his readers will read or reread Whitehead with greater comprehension and thereby possibly acquire a needed corrective to certain tendencies in current American education and in contemporary American society. At any rate, if through reading Whitehead we enlarge our scope and come to place greater emphasis upon understanding, wisdom as the way in which knowledge is held, the individual, responsible creativity, and the quest for better ways of analyzing and understanding experience, then surely we shall be the wiser for it and our educational system will benefit accordingly.

LEWIS E. HAHN

# *Acknowledgments*

THE "STUDIES IN EDUCATIONAL THEORY" series of the John Dewey Society is planned by the Commission on Publications in Educational Theory, consisting of the following members: Archibald Anderson, University of Illinois; R. Freeman Butts, Teachers College, Columbia University; Robert E. Mason, University of Pittsburgh; Harold Shane, University of Indiana; William O. Stanley, University of Wisconsin; and Arthur G. Wirth, Chairman, Washington University.

The Society would like to acknowledge its debt to Professor James W. Dye, of the Department of Philosophy at Washington University, for his helpful reading of the manuscript of *Whitehead on Education* at an early stage.

# Table of Contents

*Whitehead on Education*

# I.  Whitehead and the Modern World

THE CURRENT STATUS of Alfred North Whitehead's reputation presents some strange anomalies and contradictions. Several of his philosophic and educational writings, such as *Science and the Modern World* and *The Aims of Education,* have long been for sale in drugstores, newsstands, and railroad stations as paperback books. This was the case when such books were inexpensive and designed for mass distribution and sale, long before publishers were producing most of their lists in paper covers. Since that more recent development, nearly all the works of Whitehead are in print and readily available. Among the philosophers only Bertrand Russell has been equally accessible to the population at large, and among the educators not even the works of John Dewey have been so widely and cheaply available for so long. This sort of evidence would suggest that Whitehead is a key figure in American philosophic and educational thought.

Then the contradictions appear. Though many millions of copies of *Science and the Modern World* have been sold, obviously several chapters of that book have been completely incomprehensible to more than 99 per cent of the purchasers. This statement is not a reflection on the intelligence of the American reading public. These chapters are literally incomprehensible even to professional philosophers without the additional interpretation and insight afforded by Whitehead's other writings. Even with this help, the professional philosopher does not find them easy going. This sort of obscurity is hardly the mark of a popular philosopher.

If one asks about Whitehead's position in contemporary philosophy, the answer probably is that the majority of professional philosophers consider him something of a "period piece." It would be hard to find even half a dozen contemporary philosophers who philosophize in the Whiteheadian tradition or who consider themselves followers of Whitehead. Similarly, despite the millions of copies of *The Aims of Education* which have been bought (and presumably read) by teachers, other professional educators, and the general public, it is impossible to point to a major Whiteheadian "school" of educational thought or to find educational institutions which state that they have planned or conduct their programs on Whiteheadian principles.

Here, then, we have a distinguished scientific and philosophic figure, whose works on philosophy and education have been widely disseminated and widely read, yet who seems to have left little or no mark in either area.

A number of factors contribute to this result, some of which can be seen in connection with his rather unusual career. Whitehead was born in 1861 in Kent, England, the son of an English schoolmaster and clergyman. Educated at Sherborne and Trinity College, Cambridge, Whitehead specialized in mathematics and won recognition with the publication of his *Treatise on Universal Algebra* in 1898. The reputation based on this and his other mathematical writings was crowned by the publication, beginning in 1910, of the great *Principia Mathematica*, written in collaboration with Bertrand Russell. This epoch-making work on mathematical logic firmly established the scholarly reputation of both authors.

At this point, Whitehead's interests turned toward the wider field of the philosophy of science, and the works published shortly after World War I, such as *An Enquiry Concerning the Principles of Natural Knowledge* and *The Concept of Nature*, were examinations of the underlying concepts of modern science.

Yet Whitehead's career was far from ended. In 1924, at the age of 63, he received a call to join the faculty of Harvard University in the Department of Philosophy, and he filled that position until he became professor emeritus in 1937. This move was not a mere change of residence and institution. It was accompanied by a shift in Whitehead's interest as he moved from the philosophy of science to a general cosmology, the attempt to state and understand the totality of the universe. With *Science and the Modern World,* Whitehead began a series of cosmological works which finds its most complete and technical expression in *Process and Reality.* These later works, including others like *Adventures of Ideas* and *Religion in the Making,* are those best known to the general public.

Meanwhile his experiences at Cambridge, the University of London, and Harvard had given him direct experience with the problems of education. As an

eminent scholar he had been frequently asked to
address various professional groups or to adorn
various ceremonial occasions such as the dedication
of the Harvard School of Business. The result of
these activities is a number of essays on education
collected in *The Aims of Education* and *Essays in
Science and Philosophy*.

These biographical facts reveal some of the reasons
for the present state of Whitehead's reputation. At
the time of the publication of *Principia Mathematica,*
his work in philosophy was in the mainstream of the
logical, linguistic, and symbolic analysis which has
been the chief current of the philosophic enterprise
during this century. When, however, he turned to
cosmology, he entered what most of his colleagues
have considered a backwater. Systems and comprehensive world views are not merely out of fashion and
quaint; the cosmologist or the system-builder is seen
as one who misunderstands the proper purposes and
potential functions of philosophy.

But while Whitehead's later interests have been
unfashionable, the prevailing fashion is now changing.
Statements from many quarters within philosophy,
efforts to broaden some of the more restricted doctrines, and the rise of such movements as existential-
ism all indicate that many philosophers feel that the
scope of philosophy has been defined too narrowly,
that philosophy has abdicated its responsibilities, and
that it must return to a wider concern with human
experience than solely the linguistic analysis of propositions. While Whitehead's work may not be redis-
covered as pivotal in any such new orientation of
philosophy, his thought may eventually be less diver-

gent from contemporary philosophy than it has been
for the last quarter-century.

But possibly this very alienation from the tenor of
professional philosophy has been in part responsible
for the reception he has been given by the general
public. As philosophy became more narrow and technical, here was a man addressing himself to what
many lay readers felt were their problems and the
problems of the world. For example, though Whitehead wished to give full justice to science and its
achievements, he was haunted by the conviction that
science was not everything and that life could slip
through a net of truth-tables or differential equations.
He thus seemed to many thoughtful laymen to speak
with more insight about really important matters
than did many of his professional colleagues. If some
parts of his writings were literally incomprehensible
to these readers, other parts addressed their deepest
feelings and concerns. As a result, at the same time
he was becoming a minor figure in the professional
philosophic world, he was finding a widening circle
of readers among the general public.

The facts of biography also illuminate in part the
fate of his educational writings. Though Whitehead
served on many educational boards, councils, and committees, he was never a professional administrator
or student of the educational system. His interest
stemmed from being an educator in the same sense as
are all professors who are sincere and conscientious
about their professional duties. He never set himself
up as a philosopher of education. His educational
writings are scattered essays. He never attempted to
publish a specific philosophy of education or to train

teachers in it. Thus, in comparison with philosophers like Kant, Herbart, James, and Dewey, all of whom lectured professionally on pedagogy and were involved in the training of teachers, Whitehead was much less a philosopher of education. These facts partly account for the consequence that though Whitehead's educational works are widely read, he has left little monument in the form of specific educational theories or programs.

Yet he is widely read and often quoted. His views on "inert ideas," on the "ryhthmic nature of education," as well as his aphorisms about knowledge keeping no better than fish, are familiar to all workers in education. One may then ask why, apart from certain brief essays on Whitehead's educational position, no extended attempt has been made to use his general philosophy as a basis for educational thought and action. The reasons for this are complicated.

## II. Whitehead's Potential Contributions to Education

THE FAILURE to use Whitehead's work, beyond passing mention of certain concepts or the citing of his many quotable epigrams, is produced by several causes. One of these we have already seen: he never presented his educational ideas in one organized, coherent statement. His thoughts on education are scattered throughout his various educational addresses or appear as occasional paragraphs in his cosmological works. As a result his ideas have not been used partly because they were not easily available.

Another possible cause has been the question whether his views on education represent only scattered insights and comments or whether they actually form a coherent whole. A definite answer can be given to this question only by attempting to organize them in a coherent fashion as this volume will attempt to do; the reader can be his own judge.

That question has, however, been further complicated by one closely related to it. That issue concerns the relation between Whitehead's educational works and his other philosophic thought, particularly his cosmological theory. The most familiar and popular of his educational writings, those collected in *The Aims of Education,* were originally delivered and published between 1912 and 1928, with the majority of them antedating 1920. But it was only in 1925, with the publication of *Science and the Modern World,* that Whitehead launched into the exposition of his cosmology, the essential subject of all his subsequent books. The question immediately arises whether the views expressed in these earlier educational essays are congruent with (or even related in any way to) his more mature philosophic doctrines.

This question (although it has its special complications in regard to the specific chronology of Whitehead's writing and the particular development of his thought) is part of a still larger issue which has vexed educational philosophers in recent years: whether there is any relation possible between general philosophic theory, on the one hand, and educational theory, ideas, and practice, on the other. Whether there is any significant connection and, if so, exactly what kind of relation it is have both been matters of prolonged and complicated controversy.[1]

The present place is obviously a highly inappropriate one in which to enter this discussion, and the author's position can only be sketched in outline. But it is probably not markedly different from that of other workers in the field. Burns in some remarks accompanying his suggestions for a new analytic approach epitomizes the general position well.

> To say, then, that philosophy implies educational prac-
> tice is to say that an educator follows some set of educa-
> tional procedures because he believes certain things about
> the universe and man. . . .
>
> Educational philosophers assume, evidently with some
> justification, that there is indeed some kind of organic
> connection between philosophy and educational practice.
> This connection is of a kind that lets us in some way draw
> upon philosophy as a guiding force for our educational
> behavior, but as this analysis has shown we do not have a
> clear idea just how this phenomenon operates; we do not
> know how we get these clues from philosophy and we can-
> not explain the precise nature of "educational implica-
> tion."[2]

In short, without denying the shortcomings of present
analyses of this relation, many of us hold with another
contributor to that same issue of *Educational Theory*
that philosophy and philosophy of education are "inti-
mately connected." [3] We believe in the fact of the
relation and look to further analysis to reveal its exact
nature rather than taking the failure of our present
means of analysis as warrant for asserting that no
relation can exist.

The following pages, therefore, undertake to present
Whitehead's thought in such a way as to suggest the
maximum connection and unity of its various parts.
For those interested primarily in further work in the
analysis of the relation between general philosophy
and educational thought, the treatment can serve as
another bit of raw material or "specimen of natural
history." For those interested in the educational use
of Whitehead's ideas, this mode of presentation seems
to offer the greatest utility.

The potential gain to educators resulting from the establishment of a relation between a philosopher's general theory and his educational views can be enormous. No one writing, however voluminously, on a topic like education is going to discuss every facet of it. If we are limited to the author's verbatim statements, innumerable omissions and obscurities are certain to appear. Moreover, when many of his educational writings are directed to fairly specific problems, the task of inferring the fundamental principles which underlie his particular statements may be extremely precarious. If, on the other hand, his philosophic works present these principles and thus give the framework of his educational thought, we can be sure of our author's basic position. In addition, his general philosophic principles can at least suggest the general lines along which he would have worked in regard to some particular topic which is of interest and importance to us but which he himself never directly addressed. In short, an understanding of Whitehead's general cosmology and of how his educational doctrine may fit within it can do much to make Whitehead's thought more useful in education. Both these tasks will be undertaken in the present volume.

Nevertheless, probably the primary reason why Whitehead's work has not been utilized more is the belief that he is "obscure." This opinion is certainly not without foundation, but the difficulties which give rise to it are certainly not insuperable.

One basis for the charge of obscurity is that Whitehead never made a single simple exposition of his cosmological doctrine. *Process and Reality,* his most systematic attempt, is far from simple; and even it is not comprehensive in that he does not repeat statements made in other earlier volumes concerning certain topics, and they thus remain the definitive discussion. So, for example, he does not repeat in *Process and Reality* the extended examination he had given to the "realm of eternal objects" in *Science and the Modern World* five years before. Sometimes he also shifts his manner of presentation and even his major terms. The concept of "God" receives enormous development in *Process and Reality*, but he presents his underlying concepts in one part of *Adventures of Ideas* without using this term. As a result, it is impossible to read any single volume and thereby achieve a complete view of Whitehead's system.

Many of the individual volumes show an additional lack of coherence as a consequence of the fact they were not written as units. For example, *Modes of Thought* consists of six lectures delivered at Wellesley College, three lectures delivered at the University of Chicago, and one lecture delivered at Harvard. Similarly, *The Aims of Education* comprises occasional lectures delivered over a period of more than fifteen years. Although each lecture or group of chapters constitutes a unit, obviously this mode of composition makes each volume something less than a coherent whole. This difficulty can, of course, be overcome by the presentation of Whitehead's views in one coherent whole. Unfortunately this task has been performed primarily for those interested in Whitehead's metaphysics or his philosophy of science. Although those parts of his system which are relevant to education must overlap these in many respects, still the difference in interest prescribes a rather different type of treatment than has thus far been available to educators.

Still another basis for the charge of obscurity is Whitehead's use of a technical vocabulary. He uses terms like "nexus," "prehension," and "concrescence" which seem monstrous to the uninitiated. Actually difficulty caused by these terms is more apparent than real. The reader has to master only relatively few such terms in Whitehead's language.

In fact this seemingly tortured terminology (which is really necessary for Whitehead's purposes, as we shall see shortly) is actually a boon. The reader is given full warning that the words are used technically and that their meanings will always be interrelated in the same fashion. In this way the untrained reader of Whitehead is spared the fate of so many of those who have read the works of John Dewey. Since Dewey uses as technical terms ordinary words like "experience," "interaction," and "problem," the reader is tempted to assume that Dewey means by them whatever the reader happens to think these terms mean. The frequency with which Dewey has been distorted or misunderstood is evidence for the ease with which this mistake is made. The mere peculiarity of Whiteheads terminology sounds a constant warning, and it presents no real difficulty to anyone prepared to master a basic vocabulary of a dozen or so technical terms.

The real source of obscurity in Whitehead grows out of his dialectical mode of philosophizing and the consequent effects which this has upon the particular kind of terms he chooses and upon the transformations which they undergo. Since this manner of thinking grows out of his conception of the purpose and process of philosophizing, we can dismiss this difficulty for the moment until we consider those topics. For the present, however, it may suffice to say that this actual difficulty in Whitehead's manner of philosophizing can at least be minimized if the apparent difficulties of his diffuseness and his terminology are overcome.

At this point the educator may ask, "When we have got along thus far without Whitehead, why undertake the labor of mastering his philosophic system and his educational thought? Granted that the difficulties can be overcome, why bother?"

At least three answers are possible, any one of which is probably sufficient justification for considering Whitehead. One of these is that his philosophy can serve as an antidote to many of the ills which afflict modern education and modern society. His emphasis on individual development and personal responsibility, on fundamental theoretical understanding rather than *ad hoc* tinkering and manipulation, and on a wide range of human experience and of potential evidence about it are cases in point. The particulars of these matters will be seen when Whitehead's doctrine is examined in detail.

Second, at the present time we are far from having a plethora of modern comprehensive philosophies of education. An additional one would not be an embarrassment of riches but merely a much needed addition to the relatively small range of choice which we now have.

Third, Whitehead's system can perform two major tasks for education, which are accomplished by relatively few of the philosophies now available to us. Educators over the centuries have found themselves confronted by questions which have seemed, to them at least, philosophic, and they have turned to philosophy for answers. These questions cover a wide range and can be posed in many different fashions, but the following examples are fairly typical: What kind of a creature is man? What sort of world does he live in and what is his place in it? In what directions should education develop man's potentialities? What is the kind of life (personal, social, economic, and political) which his education should help him to lead?

Answers to this sort of question have always seemed indispensable in trying to think about education and to work with it. Parts of the answers are obviously best available from the sciences. Thus, psychology, physiology, sociology, and the rest tell us much about what man, the world, and human society are like. The educator during the past hundred years has eagerly accepted all that the developing sciences could tell him, and he has attempted to utilize this information in planning and executing educational programs. But in the long run the scientific answers have seemed to him inadequate or incomplete in certain respects, and he has turned to philosophy in the hope of supplementing them in two major respects.

The first of these tasks which the educator wishes philosophy to perform for him is to help him with the problem of value. Science has, appropriately, been descriptive and predictive. But description and prediction, however detailed and accurate, are not sufficient for education. Education as a formal process is not a natural phenomenon but a consciously instigated operation directed toward ends which are neither simple nor obvious. The educator cannot merely find and know facts; he must do something about them. He has to think about them, feel about them, and—most important—do something about them in the organization and the curriculum of an educational institution. He decides to impart or foster certain kinds of knowledge, certain attitudes, certain appreciations, and certain skills. He ignores, minimizes, or even attempts to eradicate certain other sorts. Insofar as education takes any responsibility for producing students of certain general sorts, it requires some reasons for making these products rather than others and some standards by which to judge these products. For making all these choices intelligently, the educator usually feels he needs some criteria, some standards of value, by which he can judge rationally among the competing possibilities.

The social scientist, for example, can perhaps tell the educator what values do in fact prevail within his culture—though more commonly his answer is a more complicated one which indicates the different sets of values espoused by the various subcultures within a society. But even in those relatively rare instances in which the society is fairly unanimous is the prevailing view right merely because it is the prevailing one? Or do the schools, colleges, and universities have some responsibility for shifting to a better one, if such exists and can be ascertained? Or in the more common situation, where conflicting views prevail among the various subcultures of the society is the educator merely to count noses or to assess the stresses exerted by the competing pressure groups and align his decision with the wish of the most powerful? The conscientious educator has usually hoped that

he could do better than that, and his hope of finding
some rational theory of value which will be normative
and imperative, not merely descriptive, is one of the
factors promoting his interest in philosophy. He has,
of course, sometimes been told that his hope is vain
and that philosophy can give him no help at this point.
But even if this reply is true, its educational consequences are so stupendous that the educator usually
hesitates to accept it as long as any conceivable standard of value may exist. Workers in other fields can
toy with skepticism, solipsism, or fortuitous social con-
ditioning as merely academic matters, in the worst
sense of "academic." But values are so much part
and parcel of the educator's work that he naturally
hesitates to give up hope that some rational basis for
the solution to his most fundamental problem can be
found.

A second reason for the educator's interest in philosophy is his need for a fairly comprehensive matrix
within which he can examine and attempt to solve his
problems. Though the educator has welcomed the findings of science, the very nature of the scientific enterprise renders these findings fragmentary in the sense
that they are the fruit of particular modes of abstraction from that totality of events which more closely
approximates the subject matter of education. They
are truths, but partial truths.

Each science has developed by abstracting its
chosen subject matter from the total welter of the
experienced world. Take, for example, the event of a
man leaping from a high window. Physics can study
this event and tell us certain things about it. But in
so doing, it systematically ignores, as irrelevant to

physics, many elements in that episode. Physics is not concerned with why the man jumped, how he felt at the first second after his leap, what state his organs were in after he hit the ground, or how many similar suicides daily there are in the United States. Other sciences (physical, biological, and social) find their subject matters by concentrating on these or other aspects of this total complex which we are calling the event; but, in their turn, they minimize or ignore those aspects which are of major concern to physics. In short, the sciences have usually advanced by determining what particular parts of events they shall select as their subject matter and by developing appropriate methods of dealing with the subject matter so selected. It is a commonplace that those sciences generally considered the most advanced are precisely those which are the most abstract.

Education, however, both as a field of theoretical study and as an area of practical activity, must lie close to the concrete, to the individuality of the totality of that kind of event with which it deals. As the platitude "education is as extensive as life" points out, education cannot derive its subject matter by a process of abstraction as extreme as that used by physics. The educator cannot, for example, see his students *solely* as subjects in a learning experiment, as members of various social or economic classes, as future citizens, as future workers, as family members, or the like. His students are all of these and more, and much education deals with students as all of these simultaneously. To be sure, the sciences which investigate particular facets of the student's existence do tell the educator many facts about the student, but each seems to be a somewhat partial truth as far as the educator's task is concerned. He feels the need for some means to put Humpty Dumpty together again in order to treat the student as the concrete individual which he is.

Since, however, the various sciences use different assumptions, principles, and methods, cumulation of their assorted findings into a coherent whole which does not distort the parts is not easy. The educator may juggle them into a whole by a sort of art, combining and relating the various bits of data in such a way as to give him grounds for understanding and action. But as he examines the principles in accord with which he apparently practices this art, he seems to find himself building something resembling a comprehensive conceptual structure within which these partial scientific answers can be combined and can exhibit their interrelatedness. Systematic philosophy, as the most general of the "sciences," seems to offer him an expert product of such a process of construction. Hence, his hope of obtaining this sort of matrix is one of the forces that sends him to philosophy. Once more, he has sometimes been told that philosophy cannot perform this function, but the greatness of his need makes him unwilling to abandon all hope.

By and large, these two needs—the need for some criterion of value and the need for a comprehensive conceptual matrix—are traditionally two of the educator's chief reasons for his interest in philosophy. There are, of course, other functions which the educator feels philosophy can perform for him. For example, he recognizes that its critical function can help him clarify his terms, principles, and lines of reasoning. But in part he hopes that this function will have been performed for him at the most fundamental level in regard to the philosophic doctrine which he adopts, and that by taking over its major terms, primitive propositions, and principles he will at least begin his more narrowly educational thinking with an adequate philosophic apparatus.

For such reasons as these, then, educators have continued to turn to the philosophers and have persevered in reading Whitehead in spite of his apparent obscurity.

1. Many of the contributions to this discussion are now conveniently collected in H. W. Burns and C. J. Brauner, *Philosophy of Education: Essays and Commentaries* (New York: Ronald Press Co., 1962).

2. Hobert W. Burns, "The Logic of the 'Educational Implication,'" *Educational Theory*, XII (January, 1962), 59, 63.

3. George F. Kneller, "Philosophy, Education and Separatism," *ibid.*, 44.

## III. Whitehead's "Obscurity"

WHITEHEAD'S "obscurity" is caused in part by the nature of his terms. To be sure, all philosophers and scientists tend to use technical expressions simply because such terms allow them to express their ideas more precisely and economically than do the words of ordinary speech. But, at first glance, Whitehead's terms seem to the reader meeting them for the first time even more outlandish than the usual run of technical jargon.

His choice of these queer terms is a consequence of his view of the nature and function of philosophy and hence of his way of going about the job of philosophizing. An understanding of what he is trying to do makes his selection of terms comprehensible and even helps render the terms themselves more understandable.

For Whitehead, "speculative philosophy is the endeavor to frame a coherent, logical, necessary system of general ideas in terms of which every element of our experience can be interpreted." [1] Philosophy is not one of the sciences, but rather a survey of the sciences which aims at interconnecting, harmonizing, and completing them. It confronts the sciences with each other and with concrete fact.[2] Throughout this discussion "science" should be interpreted very broadly for "it must be one of the motives of a complete cosmology to construct a system of ideas which bring the aesthetic, moral, and religious interests into relation with those concepts of the world which have their origin in natural science."[3] Not that any science gets its first principles by accepting or assuming the conclusions of metaphysics. Metaphysics and science both start from immediate experience, but in the main they proceed in opposite directions with their different tasks. "Metaphysics inquires how our perceptions of the chair relate us to some true reality. Science gathers up these perceptions into a determinate class, adds to them ideal perceptions of an analogous sort, which under assignable circumstances would be obtained, and this single concept of that set of perceptions is all that science needs."[4] Since both cosmology and science start from the same groundwork of immediate experience, they are mutual critics of each other. They should take mutual account of each other and make mutual accommodations. An adequate cosmology, therefore, includes all the sciences but generalizes beyond them, treating them in their interrelations and considering factors not adequately treated in any one science. "Thus one aim of philosophy is to challenge the half-truths constituting the scientific first principles."[5]

The ideal would thus be a single cosmology unifying the many sciences. But Whitehead is well aware of the discordant and inconsistent cosmologies offered by the various schools of philosophy and of the discredit

which has come upon philosophy because of this controversy. He believes, however, that both the controversy and the attitude toward it spring from the
"dogmatic fallacy"—the belief that philosophy is built
up from a foundation of clear and distinct ideas. The
true movement, he thinks, is in the other direction:
"the accurate expression of the final generalities is the
goal of discussion and not its origin." [6] "We are not
arguing from well-defined premises. Philosophy is
the search for premises." [7] "Our progress in clarity of
knowledge is primarily from the composition to its
ingredients." [8] The clash of philosophic doctrines
merely reveals our difficulties and our inability to
achieve those fundamental well-defined generalities
which would constitute an adequate cosmology.

   This view of Whitehead's concerning the fact of
philosophic disagreement is in accord with the realistic
element in Whitehead's general doctrine. Since there
exists for him a reality to which these generalities
correspond and which they interpret, ideally there
would be a perfect correspondence between our general ideas and this reality. But this conformity of our
cosmology to reality is an ideal which we can move
toward rather than attain. At best a system is an
asymptotic approach, a never-ending series of approximations to those general truths which we seek.[9]

   The reasons we approach rather than achieve this
perfection are several. In the first place, an ideal cosmology would give us a perfect grasp of the universe
in its totality. We would then see everything in all
its relations to everything else. But as we shall see,
these relations are, for Whitehead, infinite; hence,
such a grasp of the universe is denied us because we

are finite beings.[10] Our intuitions are hedged with
limitations and our insights are vague. For that reason alone Whitehead believes that we can never produce
a perfect cosmology. Awareness of these shortcomings
in our apprehension of reality continually suggests
further tasks for science and philosophy, but we continually improve them both without reaching perfection in understanding. As Whitehead himself points
out, however, "this notion of human limitation requires guarding," [11] and he seems to believe that the
next limiting factor is the more obvious and prior
difficulty.

   This second major limitation on our attempt to reach
an adequate cosmology is that language, our chief
instrument for recalling, comparing, and communi-
cating experience, is an inadequate tool. "Language
halts behind intuition." [12] We know more than we can
say, and we are continually realizing that our verbal
formulations of our knowledge are unsatisfactory. We
can have a clear apprehension of a general truth and
still be unable to express it adequately in words. This
feebleness of language hinders all discursive thought
because "you cannot rise above the adequacy of the
terms you employ. . . . Progress in truth . . . . is
mainly a progress in framing concepts, in disregard-
ing artificial abstractions or partial metaphors, and
in evolving notions which strike more deeply into the
root of reality." [13]

   Though science also experiences difficulty insofar
as it has to work through language and though it too
is continually seeking to improve its fundamental
analytic concepts, philosophy encounters special difficulties in the areas of metaphysics and cosmology.

"Philosophy is an attempt to express the infinity of the universe in terms of the limitations of language." [14] "But the language of literature breaks down precisely at the task of expressing in explicit form the larger generalities," [15] which is just the concern of metaphysics and cosmology.

But though terms and verbal formulations may never attain perfection, one of the tasks of philosophy is to improve our linguistic apparatus. In fact, "a precise language must await a completed metaphysical knowledge." [16]

Thus Whitehead's rather formidable terminology is a necessary consequence of his attempt to offer a new conceptual organization in terms of which we may observe and analyze experience. Old words tend to suggest only the old concepts, which, in turn, allow us to slip back into the old points of view. The new point of view is best preserved by being formulated in new terms.

A thinker who finds these limitations in language, at least in propositional, expository language, will be driven to a variety of devices to make certain that his deepest insights will be expressed in it. For example, we are familiar with the way in which teachers like Plato and Jesus used the myth, the poem, the parable, and the allegory.[17]   In my opinion, Whitehead's own favorite device is the epigram, which sometimes takes the form of a paradox. This trick of style makes his works a veritable mine of mots for almost any occasion; but it also makes his writings, as systematic philosophy, seem obscure and elusive. The reader who feels that the discussion of a topic is just about to achieve definitive statement suddenly finds himself left with an epigram. For Whitehead the epigram *is* the definitive statement. It suggests and points toward what cannot be explicitly stated. Like religious dogmas, these formulations are intended to elicit from us that "intuitive response which pierces beyond dogma." [18]

Whitehead himself sums up the linguistic difficulty in his phrase, the Fallacy of the Perfect Dictionary.[19] This fallacy Whitehead sees in the two natural, yet false, beliefs: (a) that mankind has consciously entertained the fundamental notions applicable to its existence, and (b) that it has the words or phrases to express these notions. Whitehead, on the contrary, believes that we are still lacking in many of the necessary fundamental concepts and are without the linguistic machinery to express adequately those fundamental notions which we may already have available.

Because every statement must be at best a partial truth, contexts are more important than texts, and merely piling up Whitehead's various statements about a topic does not actually tell us what he says about it. In this respect he may be much like Plato, whom he admired and followed. The impossibility of reducing Plato's view to a strict doctrine is notorious. Plato himself was the first to insist: "I certainly have composed no work in regard to it, nor shall I ever do so in the future, for there is no way of putting it into words like other studies." [20] Thus one who tries to write discursively about Whitehead is attempting a task in which the philosopher himself saw serious difficulties. A book like the present one serves primarily as something clearer than a paradox or a myth to point to some of the general truths which Whitehead was trying to suggest and to return the reader to the original works better prepared to understand them for himself.

1. *Process and Reality* (New York: Social Science Book Store, 1941), p. 4.

2. *Science and the Modern World* (New York: Macmillan, 1948), pp. 126–27. Cf. also *ibid.*, pp. ix-x.

3. *Process and Reality*, p. vi.

4. *The Aims of Education* (New York: Macmillan, 1929), p. 161.

5. *Process and Reality*, p. 15.

6. *Ibid.*, p. 12.

7. *Modes of Thought* (New York: Macmillan, 1938), p. 143.

8. *Essays in Science and Philosophy* (New York: Philosophical Library, 1948), p. 157.

9. *Process and Reality*, pp. 14, 19.

10. *Modes of Thought*, p. 58.

11. *Essays in Science and Philosophy*, pp. 94–95. Cf. also *Adventures of Ideas* (New York: Macmillan, 1935), pp. 185–86; *The Function of Reason* (Princeton: Princeton University Press, 1929), p. 51; *Essays in Science and Philosophy*, p. 159.

12. *Modes of Thought*, p. 68. Cf. also *Adventures of Ideas*, p. 293.

13. *Religion in the Making* (New York: Macmillan, 1926), p. 131.

14. *Essays in Science and Philosophy*, p. 15.

15. *Process and Reality*, p. 16; *Modes of Thought*, p. 7.

16. *Process and Reality*, p. 18.

17. *Essays in Science and Philosophy*, p. 96.

18. *Religion in the Making*, p. 144.

19. *Modes of Thought*, p. 235.

20. Plato *Epistles* vii. 341C.

# IV. Analyzing the Universe

As Whitehead says, "There are many ways of analyzing the universe, conceived as that which is comprehensive of all that there is. In a description it is thus necessary to correlate these different routes of analysis. First consider the analysis into (1) the actual world, passing in time; and (2) those elements which go into its formation." [1] Beginning with the first of these two routes, we find that "the actual world is a process, and that process is the becoming of actual entities," [2] which Whitehead also calls actual occasions or occasions of experience. These actual entities are the "final real things of which the world is made up." [3] They are "drops of experience, complex and interdependent." [4]

They are interdependent because they "involve each other by reason of their prehensions of each other."[5] These prehensions are the "real, individual, particular facts of the togetherness of actual entities," their togetherness, their relatedness, their mutual involvement.[6] Any particular set of mutually prehending entities is a nexus (the plural of which is written nexūs). These are the real, individual, and particular facts of togetherness, the mutual involvement of actual entities through their mutual prehensions.[7] These three terms (actual entity, prehension, and nexus) represent "the ultimate facts of immediate actual experience." "All else is, for our experience, derivative abstraction." [8]

Two misunderstandings can easily arise at this point. First, as Whitehead presents his notions of fundamental generality, the reader tends to equate Whitehead's terms with other words and concepts already familiar to him from some field of knowledge. So, for example, when Whitehead speaks of "actual entities," the reader is likely to equate them with "electrons," "chromosomes," or some other "element" or "smallest particle." Some such process of relating the term to a familiar concept or thing is, of course, necessary if Whitehead's term as a verbal symbol is to have any reference to items in the reader's experience. But such rough equivalents will ultimately prove misleading unless the reader remembers that, whatever equivalent he selects, it will inevitably be too narrow and too particular for what Whitehead intends. Whitehead wants his term to suggest the reader's word and more too—to be a *general notion*, including that particular term and others similar to it.

This striving for generality is what makes many of Whitehead's terms appear "fuzzy" to the reader who encounters the system for the first time. The fuzziness is intentional and necessary. A term at the level of generality at which Whitehead wants to work cannot have a clear one-to-one relation to any single particular included under it. As Whitehead says, "The only possible procedure is to start from verbal expressions

which, when taken by themselves with the current
meanings of their words, are ill-defined and ambiguous." [9] But it is the task of science and philosophy
to work continually to make these generalities more
clearly defined.[10]

Whitehead himself lived through the period which
saw the supposedly indivisible atom sundered into
smaller and smaller bits. Consequently, insofar as he
wished his term "actual entity" to suggest an ultimate
bit of the universe, he sought a term which would
leave room, not only for further advance within any
one science, but for a generalization based on syntheses between all the sciences collectively. Thus any
current scientific term is an inadequate equivalent.

A second misunderstanding is to see the three terms
(actual entity, prehension, nexus) as unduly precious
equivalents for "smallest element," "the relations between two or more elements," and "the constellation
or group formed by elements so related." This view
would be correct were the relations external, that is,
if entities existed independently in isolation and then
were externally related to other entities in a fashion
similar to the relation of the pencil to the desk on
which it lies as we commonly view the matter. But for
Whitehead the relations are *internal;* a thing *is* its
relations and its relations constitute it.

Perhaps this extremely important point in Whitehead's view should be further illustrated by taking the
case of a person. According to the doctrine of external
relations, there is an individual John Jones, who is
himself. He then has various external relations with
people and things—his physical environment, his
family, his job, and so on. But he remains the same

John Jones, merely adding or losing external relations with different things from time to time.

But according to the doctrine of internal relations, which Whitehead adopts, John has no such unchanging substance or essence which enters into relations which are merely external to it. On the contrary, John Jones *is* his relations with the rest of the universe. He is what he is because he is the father of that child, a partner in that firm, a resident of New York, and so on. As these relations change, he changes. And were it ever possible to isolate him from all his relations, he would cease to exist, for he has no essence, core, or substratum which is independent of relations. Everything is thus actually a part of all that to which it is related, and to speak of the identity and location of something is merely to specify a focal point in this network of relations which stretches through the universe.

Since the entities of Whitehead's universe are thus composed of their relations, the analysis of the universe is the analysis of those relations, the prehensions. "The analysis of an actual entity into prehensions is merely one mode of analysis of that entity but it is that mode which exhibits the most concrete elements in the nature of actual entities." [11]

The concrescence (or coming into being or self-formation or self-creation) of actual entities constitutes that process which is the real world. As a subject, the entity comes into being through feeling various data in such a way as to merge them into a final unified satisfaction, which is the entity as so constituted. The importance of this statement is reflected in the number of technical Whiteheadian terms appearing in it, and an understanding of this sentence will take us a considerable distance into Whitehead's doctrine. A few of these terms we can examine in relative isolation, but others of them will lead us out into the rest of Whitehead's system.

"Feeling" is Whitehead's term used for the "basic generic operation of passing from the objectivity of data to the subjectivity of the actual entity in question." [12] That is, the entity comes into being by treating data of various sorts offered it by the rest of the universe. This is the process of feeling; and feelings are what the rest of the universe is for that entity and, ultimately, what the rest of the universe is in it. [13]

But no sooner has this technical and abstract meaning of the term "feeling" been stated than it must be qualified by adding that Whitehead undoubtedly chose this word because he wished his term also to include the common connotations of the word "feeling." Thus the data are not merely handled or treated; they are handled in a process which has overtones of emotion, interest, and concern. [14] And this supplementary statement is as true of the entities composing a stone or a piece of metal as it is of those comprising things we usually think of as sentient.

Much the same is also true of another technical term in that same sentence, "satisfaction." Technically it means primarily the final stage of the process of concrescence, the final self-realization of the entity (in the sense of making itself real). But here, too, the common emotional overtones of the word are important to Whitehead for its use as a term. The task, the end, of an actual entity is to come to be, to create itself (in Spinoza's language, which Whitehead often borrows, to be the cause of itself). And, like the Creator in the Bible, the entity, too, looks upon its creation (itself) and, finding it good, takes satisfaction. Thus, to have achieved realization is both satisfaction in the technical sense and a ground for satisfaction to the entity in the more usual sense.

"Data" are, as we have seen, the feelings which the entity feels; they are what the rest of the universe offers as raw material to the concrescent entity. Data are of two major sorts.[15] First, there are the concrete data afforded by previously existing actual entities. The actual world is a succession of entities which come into being, exist for their brief span, and pass away. In this perishing, however, the entity, which, during the process of concrescence, has been a subject feeling the universe and enjoying its self-creation, becomes an object or superject, furnishing data in its turn for subsequent entities to prehend. Thus the perishing entity acquires what Whitehead calls "objective immorality" through this inheritance which it hands on to subsequent actual entities.[16] (This immortality is, of course, essentially like that of the germ plasm, which lives on in generation after generation.) From the other point of view, subsequent actual entities are in part what they are because of these data supplied by prior actual entities. Prehensions of this sort of data are called "physical" prehensions.

To discuss the second kind of data we must broaden our set of terms to include what Whitehead calls the "formative elements" of the universe. Whereas the world of actual entities is actual and is passing in time, these formative elements are either non-actual or non-temporal. But they are discovered by the analysis of what is actual and temporal—that is, by the analysis of the actual, real world of immediate experience.[17] These formative elements are three in number:

1. The creativity whereby the actual world has its character of temporal passage into novelty.
2. The realm of ideal entities, or forms, which are in themselves not actual, but are such that they are exemplified in everything that is actual, according to some proportion of relevance.
3. The actual but non-temporal entity whereby the indetermination of mere creativity is transmuted into a determinate freedom. This non-temporal actual entity is what men call "God"—the supreme God of rationalized religion.[18]

The second sort of data available to the concrescent entity are supplied by the second class of these formative elements, the forms. But since these formative elements are all interrelated, we may well digress to gain some minimum understanding of all of them. We can then return to the process of concrescence and see the parts all three play in it.

In the quotation just cited, Whitehead refers to this second class of formative elements by calling them "ideal entities" or "forms." These are non-actual universals, pure potentialities similar to the Platonic forms, though Whitehead often prefers to avoid all the presuppositions which cling to these terms through long philosophic use and to substitute his own term "eternal object." [19] This latter is the term which will be used in this discussion.

Each of these pure potentials is exactly what it is, though it combines with other eternal objects and enters into the composition of actual entities in various ways.

> For example, a definite shade of red may, in the immediate occasion, be implicated with the shape of sphericity in some definite way. But that shade of red, and that spherical shape, exhibit themselves as transcending that occasion, in that either of them has relationships to other occasions.[20]

The eternal objects are neither actual nor temporal. They become so by ingression into the concrescence of some actual entity, that is, by being prehended by it, and thus entering into its constitution.

> Thus an eternal object is to be comprehended by acquaintance with (i) its particular individuality, (ii) its general relationships to other eternal objects as apt for realization in actual occasions, and (iii) the general principle which expresses its ingression in particular actual occasions.[21]

Its particular individuality is its essence. An eternal object is always just what it is. This particular shade of red or this spherical shape remains constantly the same, though it is available for ingression in various modes into many different actual occasions. The mode of ingression varies, but the eternal object itself remains the same. Though eternal objects are connected with particular occasions, their essence transcends such occasions and can be understood without reference to them.[22]

If a particular shade of red is an eternal object, the total spectrum of the various shades of color must involve a large number of such objects. And similarly, if we move from spheres to other geometrical shapes, another multitudinous class of eternal objects appears. Moreover, the preceding are examples of "simple" objects. Such simple eternal objects may in turn be components of more "complex" objects, and still more complex complex-objects can be formed with other complex objects as their components. All this raises the question of how many eternal objects there are— or even, how many *types* of such objects. Whitehead nowhere explores this problem in detail. He says merely that there is an "indefinite number of types of objects,"[23] and "in the house of forms, there are many mansions."[24] Moreover, any one object has different modes of ingression into events,[25] and this ingression is subject to quantitative differences.[26] At one extreme of such difference, the eternal object may contribute its individual essence to the fullest extent (a full saturation of that particular shade of red, for example) ; at the other end of the continuum, a negative prehension may exclude that shade of red from that occasion, a relation by exclusion.[27]

The relations of any eternal object to any actual entity are indeterminate since that entity's prehensions of it depend upon the subjective form which governs that entity's concrescence, although the unique contribution of the eternal object, its essence, is always the same. The relation of an eternal object to other eternal objects is, however, determinate. "The realm of eternal objects is properly described as a 'realm' because each eternal object has its status in this general systematic complex of mutual relatedness";[28] and these relations are systematically complete. They are those relations which lie within the realm of possibility.[29] This relational essence is, however, distinct from the individual essence; the eternal object always is what it is, though in addition it has certain relations to other eternal objects.

Thus change in Whitehead's universe is not a change in eternal objects, which, as we have just seen, are always what they are. Nor yet is it change in the actual entity, each of which is precisely what it is in its definite relations to all the rest of the universe. Change occurs because of different ingressions of eternal objects into the *succession* of actual entities. Each of them is unchangingly what it is, but change occurs over the series of them. Thus change is what Whitehead calls "the adventures of eternal objects in the evolving universe of actual things." [30]

Consideration of these relations among the eternal objects brings us to another formative element of Whitehead's cosmos which he calls "God." As we have seen, the realm of eternal objects constitutes pure possibility. But not all possibilities are actualized in the world. In theory such an actualization of all possible potentiality would produce chaos.[31] Moreover, we observe that in fact all potentialities are not realized. Actual time-space is four dimensional, though many more dimensions are conceivable and, for that matter, are commonplaces of mathematical thought. The equations of physics used to describe the actual world, like $E = mc^2$, must be written the way they are written and not in some other fashion, though it is possible to conceive of a world in which the conversion of energy would be accurately described by statements

like $E = \sqrt{m} \cdot c$, $E = m/c^2$, or any other relations
within the realm of pure possibility.

Or to state the same fact from a somewhat different
point of view, untrue propositions can be asserted
about the actual occasions of nature. While fiction,
art, and criticism can use these untrue propositions
as sources of suggestion or as standards with which
the actual can be compared, natural actual occasions
do occur in certain ways and not in others.[32]

If not all possibilities are actualized, there is some
limitation on potentiality, some limitation lying at the
base of actuality. "Some particular *how* is necessary,
and some particularization in the *what* of matter of
fact is necessary."[33] Restriction is the price of value,
of existence. As an actual, though non-temporal entity,
God made a conceptual valuation of the eternal objects,
and his realization of them was in one particular pattern and not in the variety of pure possibility.[34]
Consequently,

> God is the ultimate limitation and His existence is the
> ultimate irrationality. For no reason can be given for
> just that limitation which it stands in his nature to im-
> pose. . . . No reason can be given for the nature of God,
> because that nature is the ground of rationality.[35]

This conceptual prehension of the eternal objects by
God constitutes his primordial nature. This aspect
of his nature both makes actuality possible and also
makes it what it is.[36]

But, on Whitehead's principles, the primordial aspect of God, though metaphysically necessary for the

reasons indicated, is at best a partial actuality. For one thing, Whitehead's *uni*verse is a universe in the strict sense that it is an organic or organismic whole; its parts must be interrelated. Hence, God must have some relations to the entities of the actual world of change beyond that of making their concrescence possible by his limitation on pure potentiality and beyond that of serving as the primordial "lure for feeling" or "object of desire" [37] (a function which we shall consider shortly in connection with the third formative element, creativity). If the doctrine of internal relations applies in part of the scheme, it must apply in all;[38] and actual entities must have some relation to God, and God must continually be related to the actual entities.

A second sort of incompleteness would also appear in two ways if God's nature were only primordial. For one thing his feelings would be "only conceptual (i.e., concerned with the eternal objects) and so lack the fullness of actuality. Secondly, conceptual feelings, apart from complex integration with physical feelings, are devoid of consciousness in their subjective forms." [39] If, then, God is to be fully actual and conscious, he must be united with the physical world of actual entities.

A third difficulty involved in having God purely primordial appears in Whitehead's dialectical treatment of the general problem of God's relation to the world, particularly the problem of evil. On the one hand, if he has nothing to do with the ongoing processes of the world, then he has little relevance to it. On the other hand, if he is too much in the world— if, for example, he completely determines it—the age-

old problem of the origin of evil arises. Whitehead has
no doubt that evil is real and actual and is of many
kinds.[40] If the world is solely and completely dependent upon God, he can scarcely avoid the charge of
being the source of the evil in it.

Whitehead sees at least two fundamental aspects of
evil. For one, evil lies in the fact that all that is
actual passes away. Time is a perpetual perishing.[41]
Because an entity is real, it is valuable. Value is,
therefore, lost when the entity passes away. Only
some kind of permanence amid this flux, some kind of
immortality amid this perishing, can remedy evil in
this sense. The second important aspect of evil is that
it is disorder. Evil exists where things are at cross-
purposes, where there is inconsistency.[42] If God is to
be associated with good rather than evil, he must be
associated with order as well as with permanence.

Whitehead's concept of the consequent nature of
God, therefore, attempts an adequate and consistent
solution of the problems sketched in the preceding
paragraphs. God can become fully actual and conscious only by being immanent in the actual world
and related to actual entities. He is, therefore, part
of the world inasmuch as actual entities become super-
jects and pass on their reality to subsequent actual
entities. God, in his consequent nature, is one of the
recipients of this objective immortality.[43] Thus everything does not perish completely but finds at least
partial immortality in an entity which is actual but
not temporal and is not fundamentally subject to flux.
In this way, "the immediate facts of present action
pass into permanent significance for the Universe." [44]
And conversely, God's derivative nature "is consequent

upon the creative advance of the World."[45] Because
God is immanent in the world, "Every act leaves the
world with a deeper or a fainter impress of God."[46]
But it is equally true that every act leaves a deeper or
fainter impress on God—within certain limits.

Not everything is thus saved. The prehensions of
God's consequent nature are as selective as are the
prehensions of other entities in the universe. He, too,
is internally free and determines *how* he will accept
the world. Only that can be taken into his consequent
nature which fits his primordial conceptual nature,
which remains unchanged.[47] But such elements as are
fitting do find permanence and immortality. "Every
fact is what it is, a fact of pleasure, of pain, of joy, or
of suffering. In its union with God that fact is not a
total loss, but on its finer side is an element to be
woven immortally into the rhythm of mortal things."[48]

The evil that is disorder, however, because it involves internal inconsistency, is unstable and tends
eventually to its own elimination, in contrast to God
who is self-consistent. Evil exists and takes its toll;
but in the long run and the wide view, Whitehead believes, creative action is consistent and ordered because
it is conditioned by God's immanence.[49] Evil is left
at the triviality of merely individual fact, and such
positive use of it is made as can be.[50] "This transmu-
tation of evil into good enters into the actual world
by reason of the inclusion of the nature of God, which
includes the ideal vision of each actual evil so met with
a novel consequent as to issue in the restoration of
goodness."[51]    Whitehead thus finds the foundations
of the world in aesthetic experience, because all order

(including the moral) is aesthetic and is derived from the immanence of God.[52]

Beyond this mere overcoming of evil, God is the ground and source of ideals. But these are not mere ideals at large. Those relevant to the actual state of the world, to that occasion of experience, become immanent in the world of change.[53] "Neither God nor the World reaches static completion. Both are in the grip of the ultimate metaphysical ground, the creative advance into novelty." [54]

This "creative advance" is creativity, the last of the formative principles. As we have seen, the world of fact consists of the succession of actual entities which come into being and pass away. Why is there this continuing universe of self-creating creatures? In Whitehead's opinion, there are two alternative sorts of answer. Some views postulate a Creator outside the universe who creates the creatures from nothing. Whitehead prefers the second alternative, to see creativity as immanent in the universe, as inherent in the nature of the creatures.[55] Because creativity is immanent, it does not exist apart from the creatures.[56] It is an abstract principle obtained by the analysis of actuality; it is actual only in creatures.

But Whitehead considers it important to make this abstraction because he is seeking *general* notions, and leaving creativity merely immanent in creatures would seem to limit it unduly in two important respects. One is that the very self-creation of a creature necessarily involves limitation; an entity becomes what it is only by rejecting some possibilities, by not becoming what it does not become.[57] Second, an actual entity is a quantum, but Whitehead sees a transition, a flow, from one occasion of experience to another. Creativity is protean.[58]

Generalized as an abstract principle, then, creativity is "that ultimate notion of highest generality at the base of actuality." [59] It is the motive power of the Whiteheadian universe. It is the surge, the drive toward the continual creation of new creatures, not merely additional ones,[60] but novel ones, "the infinite variety of specific instances which rest unrealized in the womb of nature." [61] Thus creativity is "that ultimate principle by which the many, which are the universe disjunctively, become the one actual occasion which is the universe conjunctively." [62] But since creativity is indeterminate, it cannot, in and of itself, effect creation. The creation of creatures is possible only when the thrust of creativity has been determined, limited, conditioned, and it is so limited by the other principles of the Whiteheadian system.

> God and the World are the contrasted opposites in terms of which Creativity achieves its supreme task of transforming disjointed multiplicity, with its diversities in opposition, into concrescent unity with its diversities in contrast.[63]

1. *Religion in the Making*, p. 89.
2. *Process and Reality*, p. 33.
3. *Ibid.*, p. 27.
4. *Ibid.*, p. 28.
5. *Ibid.*, p. 29.
6. *Ibid.*, pp. 29–30.
7. *Ibid.*, pp. 30, 35.

8. *Ibid.*, p. 30.

9. *Ibid.*, p. 19.

10. *The Function of Reason*, pp. 70–71; *The Aims of Education*, pp. 157–58.

11. *Process and Reality*, p. 28.

12. *Ibid.*, p. 65.

13. *Ibid.*, p. 81.

14. *Adventures of Ideas*, p. 226.

15. *Process and Reality*, p. 35.

16. *Ibid*, p. 94.

17. *Religion in the Making*, p. 91.

18. *Ibid.*, p. 90.

19. *Science and the Modern World*, p. 228; *Process and Reality*, p. 70.

20. *Science and the Modern World*, p. 227.

21. *Ibid.*, p. 229.

22. *Ibid.*, p. 228–29.

23. *The Concept of Nature* (Cambridge: Cambridge University Press, 1955), p. 149.

24. *Modes of Thought*, p. 94.

25. *The Concept of Nature*, p. 145.

26. *Ibid.*, p. 145; *Science and the Modern World*, pp. 233–35.

27. *Science and the Modern World*, pp. 233–34.

28. *Ibid.*, p. 231.

29. *Ibid.*, p. 236.

30. *Process and Reality*, p. 92.

31. "He is the principle of concretion—the principle whereby there is initiated a definite outcome from a situation otherwise riddled with ambiguity."—*Ibid*, p. 523. Cf. also *Religion in the Making*, pp. 94, 104.

32. *Science and the Modern World*, p. 228.

33. *Ibid.*, p. 256 (italics Whitehead's).

34. *Process and Reality*, p. 522; *Religion in the Making*, pp. 156–57; *Process and Reality*, pp. 46, 122, 487.

35. *Science and the Modern World*, p. 257.

36. *Religion in the Making,* pp. 119-20, 153-54.

37. *Process and Reality,* pp. 522, 374.

38. *Science and the Modern World,* p. 230.

39. *Process and Reality,* p. 521.

40. *Religion in the Making,* pp. 95, 155.

41. *Process and Reality,* p. 517.

42. *Religion in the Making,* p. 97; *Process and Reality,* p. 517.

43. *Religion in the Making,* pp. 157–53.

44. *Essays in Science and Philosophy,* p. 72.

45. *Process and Reality,* pp. 523-24.

46. *Religion in the Making,* p. 159. Cf. also *Essays in Science and Philosophy,* pp. 69, 89.

47. *Process and Reality,* p. 523. Cf. also *Adventures of Ideas,* p. 357.

48. *Religion in the Making,* p. 155. Cf. also *Modes of Thought,* p. 141.

49. *Religion in the Making,* pp. 98–99.

50. *Process and Reality,* p. 525.

51. *Religion in the Making,* p. 155.

52. *Ibid.,* pp. 105, 160; cf. *Adventures of Ideas,* pp. 329–30; *Process and Reality,* p. 483.

53. *Religion in the Making,* pp. 158-59.

54. *Process and Reality,* p. 529.

55. *Adventures of Ideas,* p. 303.

56. *Process and Reality,* pp. 46–47, 344; *Religion in the Making,* p. 102.

57. *Process and Reality,* pp. 66–69.

58. *Religion in the Making,* p. 92.

59. *Process and Reality,* p. 47.

60. *Ibid.,* pp. 74-76.

61. *Ibid.,* p. 26.

62. *Ibid.,* p. 31; cf. also *ibid.,* pp. 325-26; *Science and the Modern World,* pp. 250-51.

63. *Process and Reality,* p. 528.

# V. How Things Come into Being

THE THRUST of creativity finds exemplification in the concrescence of the myriad of actual entities. Just as modern physics sees energy as emitted in little spurts or quanta, so Whitehead sees the force of creativity as finding its expression in a series of ephemeral creatures, the actual entities. Actual entities come into being through utilizing two sorts of data: the physical data furnished by antecedent actual entities and the mental data proffered by the realm of eternal objects as organized through God's prehension of them in his primordial nature. These data constitute what the world is (i.e., what it has to offer as possible relations) for that organism.

The data can be prehended positively or negatively (that is, rejected).[1] But even the positive prehensions do not imply acceptance en bloc. The concrescent entity has two means of control. The first of these involves quantitative differences, the *amount* of the datum taken. As Whitehead indicated in some of the passages already quoted in the discussion of eternal objects, a great deal or a very minute amount of any datum may be taken by the entity. The second method of control is the *way* in which the item is taken, that is to say, the pattern into which it is put. So, for example, the housewife who wishes to achieve a harmoniously decorated room may find herself stuck with the colors of her furniture and rugs; yet by combining them with the proper colors in walls and drapes, she may make a harmonious whole out of what seemed discordant elements. Similarly, at the more complicated stages of art, the painter can often produce his most striking effects by the inventive combination of colors which are superficially inharmonious. So the entity which has to take data from the antecedent universe may take them in such a pattern as to mitigate the effects of those data uncongenial to it.

In spite of these means of mitigation, the evolving organism is dependent upon the situation (physical inheritance) in which it develops. A chaotic or impoverished physical environment puts sharp limitations on the possible development of the entity. And, in some fashion or other, whatever data the entity employs must be capable of eventually being moulded into a unity, which will constitute the entity as finally realized.

Exactly how these data are utilized in the production of the entity is dependent upon an important element in Whitehead's system, which we have already met several times in passing, the entity's subjective form. This form is what makes the entity what it is. It is "subjective" because it is the way in which this subject feels its data. It is "form" in that it is the unifying element in the development of the entity as a subject in the process of concrescence. Subjective forms are of many different series ("emotions, valuations, purposes, adversions, aversions, consciousness, etc."[2]), and they are what give the dominant tone to the makeup of the entity. This subjective form is not arbitrarily assumed. It is in part conditioned by the subjective forms of preceding actual entities, which are transmitted to it as physical data. There is a necessary process of conformation by the subjective form to these data.[3] Just any variety of subjective form cannot appear anywhere in the universe. The brute facts of the state of the universe at a given time and place partially determine what subjective forms are possible in that instance.

The process of concrescence begins, therefore, with the subjective form's working with the physical data handed on by the entities which have preceded it. In some cases, little more than that is involved. Thus, to take two of Whitehead's frequent examples, the entities in a bar of iron or in Cleopatra's Needle on the Thames Embankment continue to be and to pass along primarily what they originally received at the physical pole. "Enduring objects" of this sort exhibit a massive inheritance and remain what they are.

It is the prehensions at the so-called mental pole which make for novelty and change. Here the possibility of actualizing new universals appears. At a low level, for example, the Paradise fish which, having been brown with blue and red markings, mutates into an albino with pink markings is an example of such a change. The universals, the colors which describe it, have shifted. And it is perhaps worth pointing out that, though in Whiteheadian terminology this change occurs at the mental pole, there is nothing "mental" here which implies consciousness or "taking thought."

It is what the ichthyologist would call simply a genetic mutation. Any changes in the universals which characterize a series of entities are "mental."

But the conscious production of change, the desire to realize possibilities as yet unrealized, is also one of the functions of the "mental pole." True propositions about the universe such as "bread is brown" may describe the true relation at some time between the actual entities of bread and the universal (eternal object) brown. "Bread is white" may at that date be an untrue proposition as far as milling is concerned. But the man who entertains this latter proposition and tries to make it true is the person who is led to work on the refining and bleaching of flour until "Bread is white" can become a true proposition concerning some bread. Similarly, "Her hair is red and curly" may be untrue, but entertainment of this proposition may take the lady to the beauty shop with subsequent change in the ingression of redness and curliness into those actual entities which constitute her hair. In more exalted instances, such propositions such as "All men are free" or "The world is at peace," though untrue, may serve as ideals consciously entertained and striven for. As we shall see later, these untrue propositions have profound significance in human history

This mention of "consciousness" indicates that we are now speaking of organisms of complex structure. Thus far we have mainly spoken of tiny elements, the simple actual entities. But the objects of daily life— the person, the pencil, the dog, the house, and so on —consist of combinations of myriads of those actual entities. Thus if our interest is in education, when we speak of actual entities we are still a long way from such complicated systems as the student or the world in which he lives. Our problem then is how, within the Whiteheadian system, we move from these tiny particles (the actual entities) to human beings in their physical environment, their cultures, and their political states.

In general the answer is that the microcosmic process is the paradigm for the macrocosmic; or, in less formidable language, the processes of the larger units follow the model of the smaller.

Whitehead specifies a number of different types of organization. At the outset of this exposition we encountered the term "nexus," a set of actual entities which mutually prehend, constitute, and are objectified in each other.[4] Since any actual entity creates itself by this relating itself to the rest of the universe, all entities are part of some nexus and the universe itself is a nexus.

> Thus the term Nexus does not presuppose any special type of order, nor does it presuppose any order at all pervading its members other than the general metaphysical obligation of mutual immanence. But in fact the teleology of the Universe, with its aim at intensity and variety, produces epochs with various types of order dominating subordinate nexūs interwoven with each other.[5]

Thus one speaks of nexus primarily if the unity of the totality produced by this network of prehensions is not neglible and if some sort of order appears.

> When the unity of nexus is of dominating importance, nexūs of different types emerge which may be respectively

termed Regions, Societies, Persons, Enduring Objects, Corporal Substances, Living Organisms, Events, with other analogous terms for the various shades of complexity of which Nature is capable. [6]

Societies are nexūs which possess "social order," that is, have a common defining characteristic, or common element of form, which is a complex eternal object exemplified in each member of the nexus. This common form is not merely exhibited by all the members of that nexus; it is inherited throughout the nexus, each member deriving it from antecedent entities in the nexus.[7] Because of this route of inheritance which is necessary for the constitution of a society in Whitehead's sense, a society must be enduring; it has a history. Actual entities do not. They come into being and pass away. Thus the real, actual things that endure are all societies.

A society has an essential character, whereby it is the society that it is, and it has also accidental qualities which vary as circumstances alter. Thus a society, as a complete existence and as retaining the same metaphysical status, enjoys a history expressing its changing reactions to changing circumstances.[8]

Related to "social order" is "personal order."

A nexus enjoys "personal order" when (a) it is a "society," and (b) when the genetic relatedness of its members orders these members "serially." . . . Thus the nexus forms a single line of inheritance of its defining characteristic. Such a nexus is called an "enduring ob-

ject." . . . A society may (or may not) be analysable
into many strands of "enduring objects."[9]

But even at this point we are far from having achieved
sufficient complexity.

> Probably a simple enduring object is simpler than anything
> which we ordinarily perceive or think about.  It is the
> simplest type of society; and for any duration of its
> existence requires that its environment be largely com-
> posed of analogous simple enduring objects.  What we
> normally consider is the wider society in which many
> strands of enduring objects are to be found, a "corpuscu-
> lar society."[10]

All the foregoing classifications apply equally well,
of course, to organizations which are either animate or
inanimate in terms of our usual distinction.  Whitehead also uses other classifications more similar to
our customary ones.  Thus he speaks of a possible
division into six "types of occurrence in nature":
human existence, animal life, vegetable life, single living cells, large-scale inorganic aggregates, and the
infinitesimal happenings disclosed by modern physics.[11]
This classification is intentionally rough because
Whitehead feels that a sharp classification, though
necessary for science, is dangerous for philosophy
since it tends to obscure the fact that all these types
shade off into each other, require each other, and influence each other.
There is another classification, however, which is
more relevant for our purposes because it is made in
terms which are fundamental for Whitehead in that

they describe the fundamental nature of existence. Entities, as we have seen, are subjects and also super-jects. They do not merely feel data; they express them. "Expressions" and the related term "importance" grow out of this fact. Both of them involve the diffusion throughout the environment of "something that makes a difference." That is, both terms concern the diffusion, or even the imposition, of data for prehension by other actual occasions. "Expression," on the one hand, emphasizes the data as the contribution of a given finite actual occasion. "Importance," on the other hand, emphasizes the data as the immanence of the infinite world in the occasion. "Expression" thus stresses the individuality of the occasion, the particular perspective in which it constitutes itself out of the many. "Importance" emphasizes the contribution of the infinite cosmos beyond and behind the occasion, whence it arose and out of which it is constituted.[12] As a term thus referring to the infinitude of the world, "importance" is a complex and difficult term to which we will return later in other connections. But this much explanation should make intelligible Whitehead's hierarchy of "types of aggregations of actualities," which is based on the varying roles of expression and importance.

The first type is the non-living aggregation. It lacks individual expression in its parts and transmits only average expression. (Expression is thus at the very minimum since, as we have seen, expression is essentially individual.) Thus the structure of the inorganic thing survives, but such sporadic individuality as may occur in it is stifled beneath the weight of the average. The second type of aggregation is the vegetable grade, though, as Whitehead often points out,[13] it is hazardous to attempt to draw a sharp line between the organic and the inorganic. In the vegetable type, average expressiveness, concerned with the survival of the living organism as a whole, is still important. But there is some individual expressiveness of the organic parts, limited though it is by the total organism. The animal grade, the third type, is similar, but purposes transcending the mere aim for survival are discernible. (Or as Whitehead states it elsewhere, the program "to live" begins to expand into "to live well," and "to live better." [14]) The concept of importance thus has some relevance at this level. Finally the fourth type, the human grade, enormously extends the concept of importance.[15]

This extension of importance comes about through increased activity at the mental pole. "In so far as conceptual mentality does not intervene, the grand patterns pervading the environment are passed on with inherited modes of adjustment."[16] But as we move up this hierarchy of types, mentality becomes more effective; and finally in man we reach knowledge, consciously entertained and systematized,[17] and possibilities and ideals consciously entertained.[18]

1. *Process and Reality*, p. 366.

2. *Ibid.*, p. 35.

3. *Adventures of Ideas*, pp. 326–28.

4. *Process and Reality*, p. 35.

5. *Adventures of Ideas*, pp. 258–59.

6. *Ibid.*, pp. 254–55.

7. *Process and Reality*, pp. 50–51. (Repeated in *Adventures of Ideas*, pp. 260–61.)

8. *Adventures of Ideas*, p. 262.

9. *Process and Reality*, pp. 51–52.

10. *Ibid.*, p. 301.

11. *Modes of Thought*, pp. 214–15.

12. *Ibid.*, pp. 28–29.

13. E.g., *The Function of Reason*, p. 3; *Modes of Thought*, p. 205.

14. *The Function of Reason*, p. 5.

15. *Modes of Thought*, pp. 38–39.

16. *Ibid.*, p. 230.

17. *Ibid.*, p. 230.

18. *Ibid.*, p. 37.

# VI. Knowledge and Value

We thus come to two particularly human problems of considerable educational import: the problem of knowledge and the problem of value.

The details of Whitehead's theory of knowledge have less direct relevance to educational theory than one might expect. This state of affairs comes about because he construes the problem of knowledge in a somewhat unusual way. As a result, the problem of knowledge is for him much less of a special problem than it usually is considered; and hence an extremely brief summary will probably suffice.[1]

From the time of Descartes, epistemology has concerned such questions as how we obtain our knowledge of the world external to us and what warrant we have for believing in such data (e.g., sense impressions) as we think we have about it. Much epistemological thought has concerned sensation and perception as the sources of all "mental content" or ideas. How can I be sure whether the snake that I see is a real snake or a hallucination, or how can I determine whether the pink elephant I see is a symptom of incipient delerium tremens or a new biological species?

Whitehead regards this basing of epistomology on sense perception as a mistake. Instead of being simple and fundamental, sense perception is, in Whitehead's opinion, complex, secondary, and rather superficial.[2] He prefers to regard as the basis of knowledge what he calls perception in the mode of causal efficacy. This is the way in which things in fact are related by their mutual prehensions and thus constituted. This is the cosmological process we have been considering. A "real" snake (or a snake as a natural object) is what it is because the actual entities which compose the historic personal society named "snake" have mutually prehended each other and the rest of the universe as they in fact have. This mode of knowing, or rather feeling, is infallible since things are actually the way they are. And Whitehead's repeated emphasis that "we see with our eyes" and "hear with our ears" is his attempt to stress the organic involvement which underlies and makes possible sense perception.

Whitehead's second mode, presentational immediacy, is that of sense impression, and, as such, it too does not err. The mental patient who thinks he hears voices or sees snakes does indubitably have these sensations, just as the normal person "really sees" mirages, optical illusions, and the rest. But though in this mode of perception we sense what we sense, at the best, sensation is limited. There is more to the world than sense impression gives us.

The chief problems arise, of course, when the attempt is made to connect the snake as sensed with the snake as a natural object, that is, to take the sensation of the snake in presentational immediacy as evidence for the existence of a snake in causal efficacy. This linkage is, for Whitehead, the mode of symbolic reference, and it is here that falsity and delusion come in. As a cosmologist, Whitehead is more interested in the constitution of the world (causal efficacy) than in sense impression and perception (presentational immediacy) or epistemology and semantics (symbolic reference), though, as we shall see shortly, he gives great emphasis to the power of general ideas to give understanding of the world, an operation partially in the mode of symbolic reference. Nonetheless, this understanding is an understanding of the true constitution of things in human experience, and this constitution rests on causal efficacy.

If a very cursory view of Whitehead's theory of knowledge is adequate for our present purposes, rather the contrary is true of his theory of value, for his treatment of this problem is both complicated and incomplete.

In the first place, the concrescence of any actual entity constitutes a realization of value, with "realization" being used in its etymological sense of "an instance of making real."[3]   The entity, in making itself real, creates an instance of value, and the satisfaction which the entity achieves in attaining its self-creation is the primary instance of value.[4]   To be sure, there is a still more fundamental meaning of "value."

Value is in its nature timeless and immortal. Its essence is not rooted in any passing circumstance. The immediacy of some mortal circumstance is only valuable because it shares in the immortality of some value.[5]

But though the "essence" of value may thus appear to be lodged in the timeless (i.e., in the eternal objects or in God), "it loses its meaning apart from its necessary reference to the World of passing fact."[6] Hence, if value is to have any "meaning," we must seek it in the concrescence of actual entities.

The second and more complicated aspect of the value problem arises because Whitehead's identification of "to come into being" and "to be an instance of value" is only partial. Whitehead speaks of order and disorder, beauty and ugliness, good and evil, perfection and imprefection, importance and triviality, advance and decadence, and similar pairs of seeming contraries. Clearly, though all instances of self-realization are in a sense valuable, there are some distinctions or hierarchies among them in regard to their value. Though all occasions are valuable, some are more valuble than others.

The pivotal point here is, as we saw earlier in the discussion of Whitehead's concept of the good, "pattern." "Thus the infusion of pattern into natural occurrences, and the stability of such patterns, and the modification of such patterns, is the necessary condition for the realization of the Good."[7] Since the concrescence of an actual entity involves a patterning of the universe from the particular perspective of that entity and since, as we shall see in more detail later, order and disorder and other relative judgments of value also involve patterning, the study of value in both its aspects becomes a study of pattern, and the criteria of value are the criteria of good patterning.

Thus Whitehead says, in one of his later lectures, entitled "Mathematics and the Good,"

All value is the gift of finitude which is the necessary condition for activity. Also activity means the organization of patterns of assemblage, and mathematics is the study of pattern. Here we find the essential clue which relates mathematics to the study of the good, and the study of the bad.[8]

It is for this reason that Whitehead, as he says, tends to return to his first love, symbolic logic,[9] for it has predominantly that essential character of mathematics, the study of pattern in abstraction from the particulars which are patterned.[10] Of course, symbolic logic in its present state is far too limited in its scope to be useful for examining all the patterns in the universe. But

when in the distant future the subject has expanded, . . . I suggest that Symbolic Logic, that is to say, the symbolic examination of pattern with the use of real variables, will become the foundation of aesthetic. From that stage it will proceed to conquer ethics and theology.[11]

So vast an extension of the domain of symbolic logic (which would, of course, render it no longer symbolic) is a matter of the distant future.

Logic represents, however, only one approach to the problem of patterning. A contrasting and broader approach is that of aesthetics. They contrast with each other in that logic concentrates on high abstraction while aesthetics keeps close to the concrete. Logic moves from the parts to the total construction; in aesthetics, perception and enjoyment of the whole precede the analysis into its parts. Both involve the creation and enjoyment of a unity derived from multiplicity, but because of aesthetic experience's greater concreteness, it is a wider topic than logical experience and

> when the topic of aesthetics has been sufficiently explored, it is doubtful whether there will be anything left over for discussion. But this doubt is unjustified. For the essence of great experience is penetration into the unknown, the unexperienced.[12]

In sum, aesthetics, too, is not merely incomplete at the moment. For the reasons given in Chapter III, Whitehead feels it can only approach perfection, without hoping to achieve it.

Meanwhile we face the problem of making such study of patterning as we can. The problem is not one afflicting cosmology alone. Contemporary art criticism is an obvious example of our need. As art has become more abstract, the goodness of a non-representative painting clearly cannot be judged by the faithfulness with which it depicts its subject. Such pictures are patternings of colors, lines, masses, and the like; and the aesthetic judgment concerning them is the appreciation and criticism of such patterns. Aesthetic judgment can be competent only when we possess better criteria of patterning than we now do. Similarly in personality theory, the search for ideographic standards by which to judge particular life-styles or the mode of an individual life is fundamentally the search for criteria of patterning. Compensation, displacement, deprivation, sublimation, and a host of other familiar phenomena make it evident that general nomothetic standards offer little useful basis for judging the adequate or integrated personality. There can be no prescription either of the elements to be integrated or of the precise mode of integration. The totality must be judged as a unique configuration, and the problem of judging the adequacy of the integration of a personality is essentially the same as that of judging the concrescence of an actual entity.

Education, too, has long been familiar with this problem and with the difficulties in solving it. The doctrine of individual differences, for example, has been an article of faith with educators for the past thirty years or more. But as observers have frequently pointed out, it is usually hard to see any consequences of this belief in educational practices. One of the causes for this failure has been our inability to cope with the particular and unique patternings involved in individual development and individual achievement. Some progress toward a solution to this problem is one of the greatest contributions which any philosophic system can make to education. We must not, therefore, merely await the distant future when a more adequate science of patterns will be available. We must seek the best present answers to the problem and the best clues for likely directions for further search. In this spirit, then, we can examine the admittedly inadequate insights which Whitehead feels we now have.

In the cosmological writings, the two books in which Whitehead deals most explicitly with this general problem are *Adventures of Ideas* and *Modes of Thought*. In the last five chapters of the former work, Whitehead attempts to set forth the defining characteristics of "civilization," which he elsewhere calls "the ideal of the good life"[13] and "ultimate good sense."[14] He defines a civilized society as one which exhibits five qualities: Truth, Beauty, Adventure, Art, and Peace.

Truth means in Whitehead's terminology that the nexus which is the subject of a proposition does in reality exemplify the pattern which is asserted by the predicate of the proposition.[15] As the delusive perceptions prove, there is no natural necessity for such conformation. The appearances of regions may be different from the actuality of regions. But since both the observer and the observed are linked though causal efficacy, Whitehead feels there is some ground for considering them attuned together under normal conditions. Moreover, there may be a tendency, an Eros urging toward perfection, which leads to greater conformation. In conjunction with the other qualities, civilization may hasten this development. An any rate, as far as our present interest is concerned, clearly there must be an element of truth, a correspondence to reality, in the patternings of human beings and human societies. A pattern of delusions is not enough.

Beauty has several forms. The minor one, says Whitehead, is absence of clash or of vulgarity. In Whiteheadian terms, the subjective forms of the various occasions are mutually adapted and do not inhibit each other. The second kind of beauty presupposes the first but adds to it contrast of the various intensities of feeling. Thus the first form stresses unity; the second adds variety. These familiar principles of aesthetic theory are the general principles of concrescence because "the canons of art are merely the expression, in specialized forms, of the requisites for depth of experience,"[16] that is, for good patterning.

The familiar principle of unity amid variety has several well-known corollaries of a more specific kind. When we attempt to apply this criterion and its corollaries, the bad cases are perhaps more obvious than the good. Hence the point is usually clearer if we begin with the negative aspects since the positive cases often produce more disagreement.

One form of bad patterning is the result of oversimplicity or poverty. A few (too few) simple (too simple) components are combined in a rather routine and obvious fashion. Though there are no outstanding bad features, the pattern lacks interest. Nothing much has been ventured and nothing much is gained. The pattern is possibly acceptable as far as it goes. It merely does not go far.

The opposite extreme gives rise to a second form of bad patterning. A too ambitious attempt to combine too many elements in too subtle a fashion falls apart and fails to provide unity.

A third form is any attempt to combine incompatible elements which leaves the discordant elements in conflict rather than in contrast. Here again the stress on variety has lost unity.

A fourth variety of bad patterning exhibits a lack of harmony between the subordinate parts and the whole they constitute. The parts may either fail to contribute their fair share, or they may contribute too much and thus detract from the total effect. In a proper pattern, Whitehead suggests,

> each such detail receives an access of grandeur from the whole, and yet manifests an individuality claiming atten-

tion in its own right. . . . Each detail claims permanent existence for its own sake, and then surrenders it for the sake of the whole composition.[17]

To return to the positive side of the matter, then, there must be unity, but not a simple, monochromic unity. There must be sufficient variety and resolved conflict to give contrast and add interest: ". . . In syntheses there must always be a *ground of identity* and an aim at contrast."[18] Though the parts must have some individual status in their own right, they must not usurp the role of the whole. But this summary errs on the side of being too neat since, as Whitehead makes clear,

the right chaos, and the right vagueness are jointly required for any effective harmony. . . . Thus chaos is not to be identified with evil; for harmony requires the due coordination of chaos, vagueness, narrowness, and width.[19]

The summation of these familiar aesthetic principles raises, of course, the equally familiar problems of applying them. When, or in whose judgment, is a given configuration conflicting or inharmonious? These are problems to which Whitehead does not speak directly, and the second question is probably irrelevant because in his view, there is or is not a fitness of things however they may appear to any observer.

Thus far we have spoken of pattern in temporal cross-sections so to speak—at the moment of its achievement. But pattern also has a temporal dimension as was evident in the passage quoted earlier where Whitehead speaks, not merely of the "infusion of pattern," but also of "the stability of such patterns and the modification of such patterns" as necessary conditions for the realization of the good.[20]

There must be a certain stability among patterns; otherwise the result is an unharmonized chaos. In the case of biological organisms any single organism would grow into almost anything, and each successive organism would be a mutation or sport. In human societies, lack of any stable patterns would mean continual revolution. On the other hand, mere stability is not good. The lowgrade organisms exhibit this kind of persistence, the mere repetition of received pattern.[21] For development, for novelty, there must be modification within the stability. As Whitehead states it in regard to human societies, ". . . The cohesion of social systems depends on the maintenance of patterns of behavior; and advances in civilization depend on the *fortunate* modification of such behavior patterns."[22] This statement still leaves unsolved, of course, the problems of determining the optimal amount of both in the pattern of any particular combination and also of deciding under what conditions the modification can be considered "fortunate."

Much the same situation is true of two other pairs of terms: order and disorder, clarity and vagueness. "There is a natural affinity between **Order** and **Goodness**."[23] But

transcendence of mere clarity and order is necessary for dealing with the unforeseen, for progress, for excitement. Life degenerates when enclosed within the shackles of mere conformation. A power of incorporating vague and disorderly elements of experience is essential for advance into novelty.[24]

A static or changeless order makes experience mean-
ingless and reduces the universe to static futility. It
is as deadening to creativity as is too much instability.
Yet ". . . the importance of experience requires adequate stability of order. Complete confusion can be
equated with complete frustration."[25]  Yet there is
actually never *complete* frustration. "There are always forms of order partially dominant, and partially frustrated. Order is never complete; frustration
is never complete."[26]  And in historical development
there is this same interplay between order and frustration:

> There is transition within the dominant order; and there
> is transition to new forms of dominant order. Such tran-
> sition is frustration of the prevalent dominance. And yet
> it is the realization of that vibrant novelty which elicits
> the excitement of life.[27]

In one of the quotations of the preceding paragraph,
we met again Whitehead's term "importance." Earlier,
"importance" was seen as one aspect of expression
and as an important characteristic of the experience
of the higher types of organism.  In the recent quotation we saw that "importance of experience requires
adequate stability of order." Importance, then, which
has at least a partial contrary, "triviality," is something beyond both stability and order.  Whitehead is
careful, in fact, to warn us that by "importance" he
does not mean that extreme trivialization of its meaning which is often met in common usage.  In fact,
"Importance is a fundamental notion not to be fully
explained by *any* reference to a *finite* number of other

factors."[28]   If the factors are literally infinite (as they
usually are in Whitehead's cosmos), then obviously we
must be content with something less than a full explanation.

But we can get some hint of the magnitude of the
term in two ways.  The first is to look at a single quotation.  "The generic aim of process is the attainment
of importance, in that species and to that extent which
in that instance is possible,"[29] which serves to show
that importance is equated with the generic aim of
the entire cosmic process!  A second means of grasp-
ing its magnitude is to look at the "species" mentioned
in the preceding quotation, which Whitehead considers
members of this genus, importance:

> The terms "morality," "logic," "religion," "art" have each
> of them been claimed as exhausting the whole meaning of
> importance.  Each of them denotes a subordinate species.
> But the genus stretches beyond any finite group of species.
> . . . No one of these specializations exhausts the final
> unity of purpose in the world.[30]

This quotation would seem to suggest two things.
First, that after examining in detail Whitehead's
views on such major topics as morality, logic, religion,
and art, we still should not have more than a partial
knowledge of what he means by "importance."  And
second, the meaning of "importance" generically, as
well as that of these species of it, will apparently be
linked to "the final unity of purpose in the world."
In any event, "importance," like so many of Whitehead's terms, has a double aspect: one based on the
unity of the universe, the other on the individuality

of details. The word "interest" suggests the latter aspect; the word "importance" leans toward the former.[31]

Some further insight (even though partial) into the meaning of importance can be gained by examining what Whitehead says about its various species. Morality, the first listed, "is always the aim at that union of harmony, intensity, and vividness which involves the perfection of importance for that occasion."[32] Or, as he says a few sentences later, ". . . our action is moral if we have thereby safeguarded the importance of experience so far as it depends on that concrete instance in the world's history."[33] Some further clarification of "morality" in relation to "importance" and "interest" can also be gained from a passage in which Whitehead relates all these terms to the fundamental process of concrescence:

> Philosophy is the self-correction by consciousness of its own initial excess of subjectivity. Each actual occasion contributes to the circumstances of its origin additional formative elements depending on its own particular individuality. . . . An actual individual of such high grade (i.e., possessing consciousness) has truck with the totality of things by reason of its sheer actuality; but it has attained its individual depth of being by a selective emphasis limited to its own purposes. The task of philosophy is to recover the totality obscured by the selection. It replaces in rational experience what has been submerged in the higher sensitive experience and has been sunk yet deeper by the initial operations of consciousness itself. The selectiveness of individual experience is moral so far as it conforms to the balance of importance disclosed in rational vision, and conversely the conversion of intellectual insight into an emotional force corrects the sensitive ex-

perience in the direction of morality. The correction is in proportion to the rationality of the insight.

Morality of outlook is inseparably conjoined with generality of outlook. The antithesis between the general good and the individual interest can be abolished only when the individual is such that its interest is the general good, thus exemplifying the loss of minor intensities in order to find them again with finer composition in a wider sweep of interest.[34]

Thus philosophy, for example, attains its chief importance by fusing religion and science into one rational scheme of thought. For religion is concerned with particular thoughts, particular emotions, and particular purposes (though "it is devoted to stretching individual interest beyond its self-defeating particularity"[35]).

Finally, a further passage casts light on morals (as well as art) as selective:

It is the mark of a high-grade organism to eliminate, by negative prehension, the irrelevant accidents in its environment, and to elicit massive attention to every variety of systematic order. . . . In this way the organism in question suppresses the mere multiplicity of things and designs its own contrasts. The canons of art are merely the expression, in specified forms, of the requisites for depth of experience. The principles of morality are allied to the canons of art, in that they also express, in another connection, the same requisites.[36]

1. Readers interested in this issue will find the whole of the small volume *Symbolism* devoted to it as well as such passages in *Process and Reality,* pp. 238–316, and *Modes of Thought,* pp. 98–102.

2. *Modes of Thought,* pp. 181, 209–27.

3. Cf. *Science and the Modern World*, p. 136: " 'Value' is the word I use for the intrinsic reality of an event."

4. "Value is inherent in actuality itself. To be an actual entity is to have a self-interest. . . . The value of other things, not one's self, is the derivative of being elements contributing to this ultimate self-interest."—*Religion in the Making*, p. 100.

5. *Essays in Science and Philosophy*, p. 62.

6. *Ibid.*, p. 62.

7. *Ibid.*, p. 84.

8. *Ibid.*, p. 81.

9. *Ibid.*, p. 99.

10. *Ibid.*, p. 85.

11. *Ibid.*, p. 99.

12. *Modes of Thought*, pp. 86–87.

13. *Essays in Science and Philosophy*, p. 164.

14. *Modes of Thought*, p. vii.

15. *Adventures of Ideas*, p. 322.

16. *Process and Reality*, p. 483.

17. *Adventures of Ideas*, p. 364. Cf. also *Modes of Thought*, p. 86.

18. *Process and Reality*, p. 381. (Italics Whitehead's.)

19. *Ibid.*, p. 171.

20. *Essays in Science and Philosophy*, p. 84.

21. *Process and Reality*, p. 364.

22. *Essays in Science and Philosophy*, p. 83. (Italics added.)

23. *Modes of Thought*, p. 103.

24. *Ibid.*, p. 109.

25. *Ibid.*, pp. 118–19.

26. *Ibid.*, p. 119.

27. *Ibid.*, p. 119.

28. *Ibid.*, p. 11.

29. *Ibid.*, p. 16.

30. *Ibid.*, p. 16. Cf. *ibid.*, p. 37, where "the sense of morality, the mystic sense of religion, the sense of that delicacy of adjustment which is beauty, the sense of necessity for mutual con-

nection which is understanding, and the sense of discrimination of each factor which is consciousness" are named as species of importance.

31. *Ibid.*, p. 11.

32. *Ibid.*, p. 19. Cf. *Process and Reality*, p. 381: "This 'aim at contrast' is the expression of the ultimate creative purpose that each unification shall achieve some maximum depth of intensity of feeling, subject to the conditions of its concrescence."

33. *Modes of Thought*, p. 20.

34. *Process and Reality*, pp. 22–23.

35. *Ibid.*, p. 23.

36. *Ibid.*, p. 483.

# VII.  God and Reason

ALL TYPES of order are ultimately dependent upon God.  The primordial nature of God contributes to order in that it makes possible what is in fact possible in this epoch and puts sufficient limitation on pure possibility (constituted by the eternal objects) to make concrescence possible.  But God, being an entity, prehends other entities, and is prehended by them.  In this process the consequent nature of God develops along with the rest of the universe.  God in his consequent nature is, like other entities, the cause of himself and is, while externally conditioned, internally free.  He is limited by what the universe offers but is free to choose what of its offering he will accept and how he will pattern it.  Though God's primordial nature permits many different and even conflicting things to arise in the world, his consequent nature can select only those things which it chooses.  In this way God performs that function we noted earlier of preserving the good.

This side of God's nature involves, consequently, several aspects important for Whitehead's theory of value. First, since what God deems worth saving would certainly seem to be "good" in one sense of that term, the content of God's prehensions in his consequent nature should certainly have some status as good. To put the point inelegantly, what's good enough for God's prehending should be good enough for other entities. To know what God prehends would be in this sense to know what is good.

Second, if we may make the dubious (for Whitehead) distinction between form and content, *how* God patterns the universe should likewise be important. God's pattern-building should (it would seem almost by definition) be good patterning and thus should serve as a paradigm of the process which minimizes evil and maximizes good.

Third, God, in his consequent nature as an entity which rightly prehends the right prehensions, is a force for good and for value, one built into the universe and constantly available to other entities for prehension. Every other entity must, therefore, take some account of God in its own concrescence; for God, being non-temporal, need not, like other entities, reach satisfaction and pass out of existence in order to become a superject or datum. God is thus continually offering his goodness to the universe. This fact is, of course, the underlying ground for Whitehead's fundamental optimism about the course of the universe in the long run. But since each entity is internally free, this goodness cannot be forced upon the universe, merely offered.

The question then arises, "How accessible to human beings are these models which are inherent in God's consequent nature?" Whitehead's answer seems to

be that we have access to them through our moral intuitions and our religious insights. Both the words
"intuition" and "insight" are always somewhat sus-
pect. They often are used to denote some ineffable
private datum, some pipeline to the well-spring of the
eternal verities. But Whitehead seems to mean more
than this. Apparently he would be inclined to agree
that the status of any one such intuition or insight is
doubtful. Even a single set when codified and ossified
as dogma is liable to the same mistrust. But over the
ages, Whitehead feels, the total tradition is something
more than mere mass delusion. Just as any empirical
experiment, though subject to errors of measurement
and other aberrations, receives confirmation from rep-
lication by other investigators, so these insights and
intuitions, vague and illusive as any one of them may
be, do gain re-inforcement through being members of
a long and varied series. And like their scientific
analogues, their findings are corrected and refined by
later members of the set. The contribution which religious tradition makes, therefore, is primarily the
insight which it, as a totality, gives into the working
of the consequent nature of God in the universe. Thus,
in addition to the other sciences, which more obviously
work with patterns (mathematics, aesthetics, and
morals), the artistic and religious insights into the
fundamental patterning of the world do contribute a
share to our total understanding of value in the universe.

In sum, Whitehead's theory of value is far from
simple, for any system which involves, as this one
does, the mutual relations of a large number of inter-
acting variables must be fairly complex. As a result,

though we have glanced at the major terms involved in Whitehead's theory of the good, his views cannot be neatly summarized within short compass. In fact, the preceding discussion, despite its apparent length, is already something of an epitome of his doctrine in this connection. It can at best suggest some of the complexities involved in patterning in Whitehead's universe.

Likewise, it should be clear that Whitehead's theory here cannot be complete. We still know too little about types of ordering and about the criteria for judging them. Whitehead's hope was, I believe, that he had sketched out lines for further work and had indicated the immensity of the task.

One final topic demands consideration as we conclude this survey of Whitehead's fundamental views. That is the nature of reason.

> The primary function of Reason is the direction of the attack on the environment. . . . Reason is a factor in experience which directs and criticizes the urge towards the attainment of an end realized in imagination, but not in fact.[1]

The doctrine of natural selection is based on the adaptation of living forms to their environment. But Whitehead points out that animals, at least, have long been busy adapting the environment to themselves and that "in the case of mankind this active attack on the environment is the most prominent fact in his existence."[2]

This attack Whitehead sees as arising from a three-fold urge: to live, to live well, and to live better. Thus the primary function of reason is the direction of this attack, the promotion of the art of life.

At this point, however, Whitehead draws a distinction between the practical and the speculative reason. The former is "one of the operations implicated in the welter of process," "the reason shared with the foxes," "reason as seeking an immediate method of action," "a method of regulating current practice."[3]

> To its operation, the piecemeal discovery and clarification of methodologies is due. In this way it not only elaborates the methodology, but also lifts into conscious experience the detailed operations possible within the limits of that method. In this aspect, Reason is the enlightenment of purpose; within limits, it renders purpose effective.[4]

But the bulk of the little volume from which the preceding quotations have been taken, *The Function of Reason,* is not concerned with this reason of the wily Odysseus, which is enthroned above the practical tasks of the world and is concerned with keeping alive. Whitehead does not deny its importance or its utility. But, as might be expected of a cosmologist, he is more interested in the contrasting function of reason, the speculative. This is the reason which "seeks with disinterested curiosity an understanding of the world" and its function has been fulfilled when understanding has been gained.[5] While the practical reason serves the end of keeping alive, the speculative reason serves only its end, the desire to understand experience.[6] Although these two aspects are, of course, part of the same reason, must be brought together, and do, in fact, interact, the distinction remains an essential one:

Speculative reason produces that accumulation of theoretical understanding which at critical moments enables a transition to be made toward new methodologies. Also the discoveries of the practical understanding provide the raw materials necessary for the success of the speculative Reason. But when all allowance has been made for this interplay of the two functions, there remains the essential distinction between operations of Reason governed by the purposes of some external dominant interest, and operations of reason governed by the immediate satisfactions arising from themselves.[7]

1. *The Function of Reason,* p. 5.
2. *Ibid.,* p. 5.
3. *Ibid.,* pp. 6, 7, 8, 13.
4. *Ibid.,* p. 29.
5. *Ibid.,* p. 29.
6. *Ibid.,* pp. 29–30.
7. *Ibid.,* pp. 30–31.

# VIII.  Education in Whitehead's Cosmos

WE ARE NOW in a position to ask, "What functions can
education perform in such a cosmos as Whitehead has
sketched?"  As was indicated earlier, to ask this question is not to hope that by any strict logical inference
Whitehead's views on education can be derived from
his cosmological theory—that being possessed of his
philosophical works we could know precisely what he
must think about education even if he never expressed
a thought about it.  Yet to assert that there is and can
be no discernible or conceivable relation between many
philosophic views and the educational ideas and practices of those who hold them seems to many of us to
err by going equally far in the opposite extreme.  In
spite of the acknowledged difficulties of specifying the
relation, from the time of Plato on, *some* general relation has frequently seemed to exist.  What each
philosophic view has seen as "truth," "reality," "the
good for man," "beauty," and "duty," these the educational programs allied with that view have sought to
teach.  Philosophic controversies appear to have had
their educational counterparts, and educational dis-

putes have often seemed to arise from ultimate philosophic disagreement.

Quite apart from logical difficulties, the chronological situation already noted in Chapter II shows that no strict deduction is possible. Many of the important educational essays fall within the period 1912-22, but the first of the cosmological works, *Science and the Modern World,* did not appear until 1925. Clearly it is impossible to deduce the ideas of 1912 from the system in 1925 and later. Yet, to take but one example, the "understanding" emphasized in "The Aims of Education" (1916) is closely akin in nature, function, and importance to the "understanding" treated in *The Function of Reason* (1929). The hypothesis on which this book rests is that the cosmological works provide general illumination for the educational writings insofar as all are the thought of the same systematic thinker. The reader can judge for himself the degree to which the wider knowledge of Whitehead's thought is helpful in interpreting his educational views.

To help in clarifying the general relation, the following "expectations for education" have been formulated. No educational program ever knowingly attempted to teach error and perversity; they have all sought to teach the contraries of these as each sees them. To this extent at least an educator's general views impose certain limits and suggest some emphases for education from this standpoint. These "expectations" attempt to sketch in outline the general direction, at least, in which one would expect Whitehead's views to lead him.

1. *That education will be seen primarily as a process
of self-realization.* Since for Whitehead the whole
cosmic process pivots on the self-creation of the actual
entity and the development of those larger nexūs and
societies formed by these entities, we should expect
that the education of that complex personal society
which is the student would be seen as this same sort
of process. Like the actual entities which constitute
him, the student would be engaged in working out
that particular patterning of the universe which is his
educated self.

2. *That this process of self-development is a natural
process and hence one which the student undertakes
naturally.* In the cosmological scheme, the actual entity, as one of the individualizations of the general
principle of creativity, has it in its very nature to undergo the process of concrescence. Analogously we
should expect that the student would have a similar
urge to self-creation through education. Thus we
should anticipate that Whitehead's educational writings would view education as a process for which the
student is naturally ready, not as one which is foreign
to his nature and which must be imposed upon him
because of social necessity. On the contrary, the doctrine would be likely to assume that the student has
a natural bent toward education and hence may be
expected to possess considerable internal motivation
and considerable persistence in reaching his educational goals.

3. *That the task of education is to assist this natural
process.* If the student has within him this natural

urge toward development, the job of schools and teachers is probably that of guiding this process in desirable directions and of making it more direct, more efficient, less painful, or the like. But it is not a task which can be done for him by anything else in the universe.

4. *That the student would have primary responsibility for his own education and major control over it.* In the process of concrescence, though the entity cannot wholly evade matters of brute fact, it can, through the patterning it establishes by its positive and negative prehensions, control its own destiny to a considerable extent. It is what it makes itself by its process of selection and combination. In education, the student might be expected to have similar control and similar responsibility. He would determine which ones of the various educational forces which bear upon him are to be effective and what the final totality is to be.

5. *That the aim of the education of each student would be the development of a unique individual.* The whole drive of the creativity of the universe is toward novelty. Education would not, therefore, be concerned with the maintenance of that massive persistence exemplified by the bar of iron but with the sensitivity and flexibility which give higher organisms their capacity for change and hence for unique individuality. This same emphasis on individuality would probably lead Whitehead to stress the maximum development of the individual rather than his co-ordination with the group or his adaptation to it.

6. *That a major contribution of education will be that of furnishing ideas and ideals.* At the cosmological level, change occurs only through activity at the mental pole. Dominance of the physical pole produces only massive persistence, an unvarying series of similar actual entities. Only through the entertainment of new eternal objects and novel untrue propositions is any change possible, including change for the better. A primary function of education in accord with this doctrine would seem to be, therefore, to exhibit to the student models of excellence and to present new ideals for realization. This task of opening up new possibilities for realization would seem likely to be the major role of educational institutions and of teachers.

7. *That education will aid the student in judging good patterns.* Truistically, any educational program based on a philosophic system will try to enable the student to achieve "the good" as it is defined by that system. Since Whitehead's fundamental criteria are aesthetic, the essential goodness of anything will lie in the fact that it is an instance of good patterning. Although Whitehead believes that human experience and human reflection do not yet offer us complete formulas for judging all sorts of ordering, making available to the student such incomplete insights as we now possess seems clearly a likely task for his educational program. Thus we might expect considerable emphasis on the criteria of good patterning, on examples of good pattern, and the like.

8. *That education will attempt to help the student effect these changes and achieve these ideals.* White-

head clearly believes in the necessity of making the good real and is well aware of the problems involved in so doing. Merely to entertain good ideas or to conceive high ideals is not enough. They must be actualized in the world. Hence we should expect that education in accord with this doctrine would give major emphasis to promoting the student's ability to make these possibilities real, to be effective in the world. Thus competence in science and technology, in problem-solving, in persuasion, and in other means of achieving such transformations would seem likely objectives for education.

9. *That, though the development of the practical reason will thus be stressed, still greater emphasis will fall on the development of the speculative reason.* Inasmuch as "the function of Reason is to promote the art of life," the development of this capacity would seem an obvious concern of education. And though, as we have just seen, Whitehead clearly will never belittle the necessity for solving life's problems nor the value of the skills involved in making the ideal real, he will probably attach still greater importance to the development of the speculative reason. Thus we should expect his educational program to give special attention to the speculative reason which aims at understanding experience, in contrast to the practical reason which solves the immediate problems which experience presents. And since the speculative reason finds delight in the functioning of its own powers rather than in achieving practical solutions to problems, we should expect a curriculum which stresses his speculative

comprehension of the universe and one in which the student is to be interested because of his interest in understanding his experiences rather than in solving his immediate problems, however pressing.

10. *That the educated man and educational programs, like everything else in the Whiteheadian universe, will be judged on the basis of the particular totality each of them constitutes.* That is, we should not expect that there would be inherently good or indispensable elements in the personality or the curriculum whose mere presence would in themselves make a person or a program good. Nor should we expect some particular educational pattern to be suggested, one that would be good for all persons, times, places, and educational contents. Rather we should expect that each person and program will be judged on the basis of whether it constitutes the best possible patterning of all those mutual relations which are the particular student and the rest of his universe.

These "expectations" are admittedly general, but they do serve to delineate the major outlines of a particular view of the educational process and educational programs, a view clearly different from others past and present. If Whitehead's explicitly educational writings are generally consonant with his philosophical position, then his educational remarks will be in general accord with these propositions, adding greater detail and specificity to them. Thus these propositions can serve as a bridge by which we can move from Whitehead's cosmological views to his specifically educational writings.

## IX.  The Aims of Education

IN SEEKING Whitehead's views concerning the ends of education, the most useful starting point is the early essay entitled "The Aims of Education," which also gives its title to the book of which it is the first chapter. In this essay the strand of Whitehead's thought on this topic is woven of a number of different skeins; and the concepts in each thread are subjected to considerable verbal variation in statement. But I believe this is a variety of expression rather than of fundamental thought. Hence I shall begin by following each of these seemingly different lines of thought, adding such material from his other writings as will supplement or explain the comments of this essay. Only later will an attempt be made to look for relation among them.

Whitehead sees as the general context of his problem the fundamental uncertainty in English education as to whether it should produce amateurs or experts.[1] It is in this light that Whitehead's statement at the outset of this essay is to be understood—i.e., that we should aim at producing men who possess both culture

and expert knowledge in some direction. What Whitehead means by "culture" he partially explains in the
first sentence: it is "activity of thought and receptiveness to beauty and human feelings."[2]  The amateur is
thus the man of culture and appreciation (i.e., who is
receptive to beauty and humane feeling), capable of
activity of thought, and versatile in mastering any
given routine. The expert, on the other hand, has the
power and the foresight which come from specialized,
expert knowledge. The goal of education is to produce
the person who combines both.

Foresight has a part in making education "religious"—and it is the essence of education that it be
religious "when it inculcates duty and reverence."
"Duty arises from our potential control over the
course of events.  Where attainable knowledge could
have changed the issue, ignorance has the guilt of
vice."[3]  Insofar, then, as specialized knowledge enables
us to know our duty and to do it, specialized knowledge, and it alone, contributes this part of the essence
of education.[4]

In this same essay the aims of education are also
stated in different wording, as follows: "What education has to impart is an intimate sense for the power
of ideas, for the beauty of ideas, and for the structure
of ideas, together with a particular body of knowledge
which has peculiar reference to the life of the being
possessing it."[5] The first of these objectives (an intimate sense for the power of ideas) is not further developed in this phraseology within this first lecture,
though I believe that Whitehead's remarks on "important" and "non-inert" ideas (which we shall examine
in a moment) clearly are intended by him to be expli-

cations of this point.[6] The second element, a sense for the beauty of ideas, is probably only a particular instance of that general aesthetic sensibility claimed for the amateur as the result of his general education. The third, the appreciation for the structure of ideas, can develop only under the influence of special study, "for only it can give an appreciation for the exact formulation of general ideas, for their relations when formulated, for their service in the comprehension of life."[7] The fourth element, the particular body of knowledge, appears to consist primarily of that "expert knowledge in a given direction" which is the possession of the specialist, though the amateur, too, has a body of knowledge relating to his "culture."

In short, of the four aims of education mentioned in this statement, only the second seems clearly the province of the cultivated amateur, though he has some share of all but the third; the specialist, on the other hand, has clear claim to the first, second, and fourth.

The general line of thought, which we have seen Whitehead developing in his treatment of "foresight," "duty," and "the service of general ideas in the comprehension of life," receives its most impressive treatment in his discussion of "style." The sense of style is the most austere of all mental qualities, "It is an aesthetic sense, based on admiration for the direct attainment of a foreseen end, simply and without waste. . . ."[8] Style is the exclusive privilege of the expert, the product of the specialist and the peculiar contribution of specialism to culture. Style is not merely the attainment of one's end. That is power. Though power itself is fundamental, style is the fashioning and restraining of power. Style adds the aesthetic quality that the end is attained directly, simply, and without waste. Style is thus the ultimate morality of mind. "With style you attain your end and nothing but your end. With style the effect of your activity is calculable, and foresight is the last gift of gods to men."[9] Thus style is moral because it sharpens foresight; it shows us our duty and enables us to perform it by controlling the course of events.[10]

Despite the fact that style may be said to be the exclusive privilege of the expert and to be the peculiar contribution of specialized study, there is a related contribution from general education or general culture. "Art and literature have not merely an indirect effect on the main energies of life. Directly, they give vision. . . . Vision is the necessary antecedent to control and to direction."[11]  If, then, style enables us to effect our ends, there must be some source of direction concerning which ends we should seek. Or, as Whitehead states it: "The aim of education is the marriage of thought and action. . . . And beyond both there is the sense of what is worthy in thought and worthy in action."[12]

Consideration of style brings us to another main strand in Whitehead's educational thought, the conviction that education must be useful. Style is not only the last acquirement of the educated mind; it is also the most useful.[13] Of course, says Whitehead, all education must be useful; it is useful because education gives understanding, and understanding is useful.[14] "Understanding" is thus a rather pivotal term for Whitehead, and he is careful to explain it here and in his other writings. Whitehead wants the student to get "an understanding of that stream of events which pours through his life, which is his life."[15] And this understanding is given by the grasp of a few important ideas which the student can make his own and can see applied in the circumstances of his actual life.[16]

It seems evident, therefore, that "understanding" here is identical with the "understanding" we met earlier, that function of the speculative reason which "seeks with disinterested curiosity an understanding of the world. Naught that happens is alien to it. It is driven forward by the ultimate faith that all particular fact is understandable. . . ."[17] And certainly the relation of these uses of "understanding" to that employed in his definition of metaphysics should not be ignored: "By 'metaphysics' I mean the science which seeks to discover the general ideas which are indispensably relevant to the analysis of everything that happens."[18]

We gain further information regarding these "important" ideas which contribute to this understanding if we consider their contraries, "inert ideas." The whole essay, "The Aims of Education," and indeed the whole book (as Whitehead makes clear in the Preface) are devoted to an attempt to free education from the weight of inert ideas, "ideas that are merely received into the mind without being utilized, or tested, or thrown into fresh combinations."[19]

If we consider the last of these three charactertistics ("thrown into fresh combinations"), we immediately see that we have another parallel to Whitehead's fundamental metaphysical doctrine. Creative novelty is the end of the universe, and this novelty depends upon concrescences controlled by novel patterns of relevance. That education should be a source of suggestion for such novel patterns would seem a clear expectation; and so we find it developed in Whitehead's educational plans. We have already seen how this ability to acquire new ideas apparently leads to versatility in mastering routines[20] and how seemingly alien ideas can lead to greater fertility of thought when they are applied to some new field.[21] It is this extension of generalizations from one field to another which is a basic element in those "imaginative rationalizations" which are a fundamental tool of speculative philosophy.[22]

"Imagination" and "adventure," which we encountered as important terms in Whitehead's cosmology, also figure largely in his educational thought. Imaginative functioning is of several different types. One type is strengthened by poetic literature; another by scientific training. "If we are finally to sum up in one phrase the peculiar impress on character to be obtained from a scientific training, I would say that it is a certain type of instinctive direction in thought and in observation of nature, and a facility of imagination in respect to the objects thus contemplated, issuing in a stimulus toward creativeness."[23] If knowledge is conventionalized in orthodoxies, the possibilities for novelty are lost. It is for this reason that learning must be "lighted up with imagination."[24] Otherwise that adventure which goes beyond the past and which produces novelty is impossible.[25] This adventure demands that the connection between knowledge and the zest for life be preserved, and this can be done by uniting at the university old and young in the imaginative consideration of learning, welding together imagination and experience.[26]

Related to imagination and apparently assisting in evoking it are the various forms of "suggestiveness." There is the suggestiveness of learning arising from the contemplation of orthdox expositions and orthodox experiment. But there is another suggestiveness derived from brute fact as it is encountered in the law, religion, medicine, business, art, education, and government.[27] Suggestiveness, then, will aid imagination, which will throw important ideas into fresh combinations and thus produce novelty which makes possible that adventure which, as we saw in the preceding chapter, is one of the marks of civilization.

The second characteristic of a "non-inert" idea, that it be "tested," is a complex matter. Whitehead, as he says, extends the meaning of "prove." He accepts, of course, the narrower meaning of "proof" in the sense of "the proof, either by experiment or logic, of the truth of the proposition." His extension of the meaning, however, is "prove" in the sense of proving the idea's worth, appreciating its importance.[28] This is "appreciation by use" and is essentially the same thing as the remaining characteristic of the non-inert idea, that it be "utilized."

Utilization is not meant in any narrow sense either. "By utilizing an idea, I mean relating it to that stream, compounded of sense perceptions, feelings, hopes, desires, and of mental activities adjusting thought to thought, which forms our life."[29] This is utilization in a sense very close to "understanding." These ideas which are utilized need not solve immediate problems; they merely make sense out of life. They offer a potential matrix for that "possible harmony of diverse things."[30]    Like Aristotle, Whitehead, as we shall later see in more detail, believes that all men by nature desire to know; hence any idea that leads to understanding will be considered useful by man.

Whitehead's meanings for "application" and "utilization" merit considerable emphasis since they differ rather sharply from the meanings often employed for these words by other educators.    For example, Newton's laws may be applied to the planetary motions; but some educators would question whether such "theoretical" or "abstract" knowledge could be called useful unless it helped the student achieve some immediate purpose, solve some problem, or the like.    For Whitehead the knowledge of Newton's laws is useful to the student because such knowledge gives him intellectual understanding of the world which surrounds him. "Practice" for Whitehead, therefore, can consist in the application of these laws to planetary motions. "Proof" (in the narrower sense) of this practical application would consist of the observations or experiments which would indicate that the laws are applicable.    "Proof" in Whitehead's extended sense would consist in the student's realization of how many varied natural phenomena are explicable by these laws. Theory for Whitehead would be the statement of the laws themselves, their mathematical formulation; and proof of the theory would be largely logico-mathematical.

Whitehead maintains a distinction between proof and utilization; but in the educational process he believes there should be a continual interplay between them—yet this interplay should not result in the student's becoming confused as to which is which.[31]    For it is only by application or utilization that theory gains meaning.[32]

One other important thread of Whitehead's thought about aims remains to be examined. We saw earlier that it is the essence of education to be "religious" in Whitehead's sense; and we saw how the specialist's foresight enables him to control the course of events and thus to see and do his duty. But, in addition to duty, religion involves the inculcation of reverence. The foundation of reverence is the perception that "the present holds within itself the complete sum of existence, backwards and forwards, that whole amplitude of time which is eternity."[33] This emphasis on the present is a common theme in Whitehead's writings and one which has obvious connections with his doctrine of the mutual immanence of things and the continuity of experience. So, early in the essay on "aims," he states: "The understanding which we want is an understanding of the insistent present. The only use of knowledge of the past is to equip us for the present. . . . The present contains all that there is. It is holy ground; for it is the past and it is the future."[34] Because of his numerous references to the importance of the present and to the importance of freshness in knowledge, some have been tempted to push Whitehead into a cult of presentism, which would hold that the present is the *only* important thing. But as he himself says: "We cannot get rid of the past so easily. For if the past be irrelevant to the present, then the present and the understanding of it go together with the relevance of the present to the future."[35] To be sure, only the actual entities of the present moment are actual; they are the real things amid the flux of experience.

But though the reality of present actual entities does give them a certain standing, the real things are not the only important elements of the cosmos. They are what they are only because of data they have received from the past and they are important because they are the seeds of the future—which is not yet real. The eternal objects, too, are important, though they are not real except as realized in present actual entities. We cannot understand the universe unless we understand the here and now. But to understand the present we must see it as being derived from the past and as having consequences for the future. "Hence it is the business of a sound education to strengthen this sense of derivations and consequences, and to provide it with understanding."[36]

Thus, that part of religion which is reverence is partially a result of general education and is not, like duty, almost solely the product of specialized study. General understandings and a receptiveness to beauty and to humane feelings would seemingly play no small part in enabling us to see the present in its proper perspectives and thus to achieve part of the essence of education.

As the climax and also the unification of all that has gone before comes wisdom. It is clearly Whitehead's major educational term, resting on and controlling all the other elements we have seen thus far.

Wisdom is the way knowledge is held. It concerns the handling of knowledge, its selection for the determination of relevant issues, its employment to add value to our immediate experience. This mastery of knowledge, which is wisdom, is the most intimate freedom obtainable.[37]

"Wisdom should be more than intellectual acuteness. It includes reverence and sympathy, and a recognition of those limitations which bound all human endeavor."[38] As is usual with Whitehead, this important term is to be understood in both the individual perspective and in a larger one. On the individual side, "Wisdom is the fruit of balanced development. It is this balanced growth of individuality which it should be the aim of education to secure."[39] And on the social side, "A living civilization requires learning, but it lies beyond it."[40] It is this culminating and directing role of wisdom which best explains that statement of Whitehead which we saw earlier: "The aim of education is the marriage of thought and action. . . . And beyond both there is the sense for what is worthy in thought and worthy in action."[41]

The preceding analysis of Whitehead's views concerning the ends of education by following the separate strands may have given the impression that it is not a unified whole. But Whitehead's own connection between many of these apparently separate threads—connections apparent even in the fragments just quoted in isolation—and his interweaving of many of his major terms suggest that this is merely one form of the problem of the one and the many and that Whitehead is attempting to express an organically unified view. As Whitehead would be the first to point out, any verbal statement of such a view must of necessity be inadequate, but perhaps the following statement will at least suggest more and different relations between the parts than the connections we have already seen. And to suggest the maximum possible relation between Whitehead's educational thought and his cosmological theory, I shall couch this statement fundamentally in the terms of that theory, adding the educational content to it.

As a developing organism, the human being has experience in its twofold aspect, feeling and expression: he receives and integrates what the circumambient universe has to offer; he leaves his impress on that universe. This is true of all actual entities and nexūs. But the society which is a human being, because of greater activity at the mental poles and because ideas and ideals can be consciously and imaginatively entertained, can be more creative in this act of self-constitution (and hence is more educable) than is, say, a bar of iron. Moreover, the human being wishes, not merely to live, but to live better and to live well.

We see, then, that certain characteristics that education aims to develop all increase enormously the range, variety, and quality of the feelings to which the organism is receptive: "appreciation"; "sensitivity to humane feelings," to "poetry which is beyond philosophy and science," to art, which sharpens the senses and goes beyond them; "versatility," the habit of entertaining notions of adequate generality"; "fertility of thought"; the "sense for the power, beauty, and structure of ideas"; "vision"; and "reverence."

In regard to expression, "power," "style," and "duty" (which are predominantly outcomes of specialized knowledge) all aid in that "diffusion of something that matters" and in that "conquest of the environment" which is expression. Thus the many and varied "aims" stated for education can all be seen as contributing to the two aspects of experience, feeling and expression. But it is the total education of one organism which strives for unity. And presiding over the entire operation should be "understanding" (which throughout the entire process should enable the organism to see itself in relation to the rest of the universe and to perceive the particular facts of its own experience as exemplifications of general laws) and "wisdom" (that "fruit of the balanced development" which gives the sense of "what is worthy in thought and worthy in action").

The concrescence of a simple actual entity is complicated because that process has aspects, stages, or moments as the entity copes in various ways with the various elements of the universe presented to it. The development of that conscious society which is a human being is still more complicated because of the variety and subtlety of relations within itself and with the world. Education, which is connected with this process, tends itself, therefore, to have moments or aspects which correspond to parts of this process and hence has the variety of aspects which Whitehead touches upon. But through separable analytically, these aspects of education are not actually separate any more than are the various stages or aspects of concrescence. *The aim* of education is to enable the human organism to effect, through adventure, that sort of self-creation which will be a good patterning of the data available in that epoch and which will constitute a creative advance into novelty.

But whether stated in cosmological or educational

terms, the views of Whitehead concerning the ends of education are, when couched at this level of generality, similar to those of other educators. Educational generalizations tend inevitably to be platitudinous. We must wait to see the more specific meaning Whitehead will give to these general statements by his more particular comments on method and content as related to the various aims. Even at this level of generalization, however, two fairly distinctive features are apparent. One is his emphasis on unity or integration, not simply as a desirable result, but as a necessity lying in the nature of things. The second is his emphasis on understanding as an innate desire of the individual to understand his experience and to see himself in relation to the rest of the cosmic process.

1. *The Aims of Education,* p. 20.

2. *Ibid.,* p. 1. The contrast is further sharpened and clarified in *Science and the Modern World,* p. 285: "The makeweight which balances the thoroughness of the specialist intellectual training should be of a radically different kind from purely intellectual analytical knowledge."

3. *The Aims of Education,* p. 23. Cf. *Essays in Science and Philosophy,* p. 157: "Knowledge is a process, adding content and control to the flux of experience." Whitehead has no doubts that specialized knowledge and training are the bases of the curriculum. In fact, Whitehead would like to increase the amount of specialization possible, provided the cost is not "minds in a groove" (*Science and the Modern World,* p. 285).

4. As we shall see later, this emphasis on the uniqueness of this contribution of specialized knowledge is subject to qualification at a higher level.

The part which "reverence" plays in the essence of education will be discussed *infra,* pp. 99–100.

5. *The Aims of Education,* p. 18.

6. The value of ideas from other fields when applied to any given field of specialization (*ibid.,* p. 82) and also the point that specialized knowledge is effective knowledge (*Science and the Modern World,* p. 282) have already been noted.

7. Very similar to this statement are the goals indicated for mathematical instruction in "The Mathematical Curriculum": The pupils should acquire familiarity with abstract thought, should realize how it applies to particular concrete circumstances, and should know how to apply general methods to its logical investigation (*The Aims of Education*, p. 120).

8. *Ibid.*, p. 19.

9. *Ibid.*, pp. 19–20.

10. Cf. *ibid.*, p. 23.

11. *Ibid.*, p. 91.

12. *Essays in Science and Philosophy*, p. 127.

13. *The Aims of Education*, p. 19.

14. *Ibid.*, p. 3.

15. *Ibid.*, p. 3.

16. *Ibid.*, p. 3. Cf. "Our goal is to see the immediate events of our lives as instances of our general ideas" (*ibid.*, p. 79). Thus the function of the university is "the discovery, the understanding, and the exposition of the possible harmony of diverse things," and the understanding, insofar as one is possible, of that fundamental problem of the relation of the one to the many (*Essays in Science and Philosophy*, p. 164). Cf. also *The Aims of Education*, p. 157.

17. *The Function of Reason*, p. 29.

18. *Religion in the Making*, p. 84.

19. *The Aims of Education*, pp. 1–2. The same general view is expressed in "The Mathematical Curriculum," in which Whitehead points out that what must be avoided is the "pointless accumulation of details" and that what must be stressed are those relations of number, quantity, and space which are "of fundamental importance" (*ibid.*, pp. 121–22). Cf. also *Essays in Science and Philosophy*, p. 147.

20. *The Aims of Education*, pp. 22–23.

21. *Ibid.*, p. 82; *Science and the Modern World*, pp. 282–86.

22. *Process and Reality*, pp. 7–8.

23. *Essays in Science and Philosophy*, p. 144.

24. *The Aims of Education*, p. 146. Cf. also *Essays in Science and Philosophy*, pp. 23–24.

25. *Adventures of Ideas*, pp. 360 ff. "Inconsistent truths are . . . seed beds of suggestiveness. The progress which they suggest lies at the very root of knowledge."—*Essays in Science and Philosophy*, p. 159.

26. *The Aims of Education,* p. 139.

27. *Essays in Science and Philosophy,* p. 162. For the universities not to miss the suggestiveness inherent in brute fact, they must keep in close touch with vocational practices. One educational consequence of this position, as we shall see later, is that the proper educational curriculum would synthesize the traditional literary, scientific, and technical curricula.

28. *The Aims of Education,* pp. 4–5.

29. *Ibid.,* p. 4. Whitehead is not, of course, opposed to "utility" in a narrower sense. Skill in writing, spelling, and arithmetic, a command of French, and the like are all acknowledged to be useful acquirements (*ibid.,* pp. 35, 99).

30. *Essays in Science and Philosophy,* p. 164.

31. "What is proved should be utilized, and what is utilized should—as far as practicable—be proved. I am far from asserting that proof and utilization are the same thing."—*The Aims of Education,* p. 6.

32. "In fact, the applications are part of knowledge. For the very meaning of things known is wrapped up in their relationships beyond themselves. Thus unapplied knowledge is knowledge shorn of its meaning."—*Essays in Science and Philosophy,* p. 161. Cf. also the statement (in *The Aims of Education,* p. 74) that mathematics, especially for the child, is mere verbiage without shopwork practice in application.

33. *The Aims of Education,* p. 23.

34. *Ibid.,* pp. 3–4.

35. *Essays in Science and Philosophy,* p. 151.

36. *Ibid.,* p. 151.

37. *The Aims of Education,* p. 46.

38. *Essays in Science and Philosophy,* p. 125.

39. *Science and the Modern World,* p. 284.

40. *Adventures of Ideas,* p. 360.

41. *Essays in Science and Philosophy,* p. 127.

# X.  The Rhythm of Learning

ONCE ONE HAS abstracted "aims" from the rest of the educational process, the second most fundamental concept in giving structure to Whitehead's educational thought is his doctrine of the "rhythmic" nature of learning. This rhythm involves what is taught, when it is taught, and how it should be taught. Whitehead's doctrine of rhythm is set forth chiefly in two essays in *The Aims of Education*, "The Rhythm of Education" and "The Rhythmic Claims of Freedom and Discipline," which constitute the main sources for the following summary of his views.

In the first of these essays, Whitehead is seeking some principle by which the sequence of subjects in the curriculum can be ordered. The principle which he wishes to propose is that "different subjects and modes of study should be undertaken by pupils at fitting times when they have reached the proper stage of mental devolpment."[1] Whitehead believes that this is a truism which everyone knows and accepts, but he doubts whether this truth has ever been handled in educational practice with due attention to the psychology of the pupil.

At the outset Whitehead is careful to deny two principles often used in deciding the curricular sequence of subjects because both of them appear to be in accord with the truistic principle just stated. The first of these rejected interpretations is that the easier subjects should precede the harder ones. It might seem as if this principle could be translated into Whitehead's statement by saying that the easier tasks are best fitted to the earlier stages of mental development and the harder tasks to the later stages. But as Whitehead sees it, this order is in fact often reversed "because nature so dictates and because they (the harder subjects) are essential to life."[2] Thus nature dictates that the first intellectual task which confronts the infant is the acquisition of the spoken language, an appalling task. Yet the fact that every child manages to perfom this miracle seems to Whitehead sufficient reason for stopping nonsensical talk about postponing the harder subjects. If any further evidence is needed, Whitehead feels it can be found in the fact that the study of the elements of algebra, which Whitehead considers the most difficult part of mathematics, must necessarily precede the comparative simplicity of differential calculus.

The second of these examples suggests the other plausible, but dubious, principle of curricular sequence, necessary precedence. In some instances, as in the case of the necessary priority of algebra to calculus, Whitehead believes this principle is sound; but he thinks that its universal application is possible only by a very artificial limitation in the concept of "a subject for study." In one sense, of course, it is true that you cannot read Homer until you can read, or perhaps even until you have learned to read, ancient Greek. But, as Whitehead points out, Homer was originally recited by a bard to audiences which were illiterate, and through the ages many children have heard the tale of the wanderings of Odysseus long before they could read. Thus whether Homer is a suitable subject for study in the kindergarten or the graduate seminar depends upon how Homer as a subject for study is defined.[3]

Thus two principles, that of order of difficulty and that of necessary precedence, are explicitly dismissed. They resemble the kind of principle which Whitehead seeks, but both of them are overly concerned with relations between subject matters and insufficiently concerned with the relation between the subject matter and the student. In view of Whitehead's doctrine of mutual immanence, this sort of objection was to be expected.

Once we come to consider the nature of the learner and his learning, Whitehead sees as the commonest misconception the belief that the student's progress is a steady, uniform advance from the elementary stages of the subject to the most advanced level which the student attains, a movement containing no changes in the kind of progress and no changes in pace. In contrast, Whitehead sees this move as cyclic, periodic, rhythmic. Life is that way,[4] and education, being part of life and having life as its subject, will be the same. This rhythmic character of education also affects its aims, though our previous discussion ignored this fact. "The aims of education are not mystical and far-off. The student must be continually enjoying some fruition and starting afresh." [5]

Whitehead believes that this periodic or cyclic nature of life and of education was correctly analyzed by Hegel into the stages of thesis, antithesis, and synthesis; but in applying this analysis to education Whitehead prefers to call the stages those of romance, precision, and generalization.

In the stage of romance, "the subject-matter has the vividness of novelty; it holds within itself unexplored connections with possibilities half-disclosed by glimpses and half-concealed by the wealth of material."[6] "It is a process of discovery, a process of becoming used to curious thoughts, of shaping questions, of seeking for answers, of devising new experiences, of noting what happens as the result of new ventures."[7] This first experience with subjects is not, however, completely unchanneled. "In no part of education can you do without discipline or can you do without freedom; but in the stage of romance the emphasis must always be on freedom, to allow the child to see for itself and to act for itself."[8] There must be discipline since discipline gives order. But by and large the aim during the period of romance is to make the child like Adam—i.e., to give him a chance to see the animals before he is required to name them."[9]

> But when this stage of romance has been properly guided, another craving grows. . . . The freshness of inexperience has worn off; there is a general knowledge of the groundwork of fact and theory; and, above all, there has been plenty of independent browsing amid firsthand experiences, involving adventures of thought and of action. The enlightenment which comes from precise knowledge can now be understood.[10]

In this second stage of precision, "width of relation-

ship is subordinated to exactness of formulation. . . .
New facts are added, but they are facts which fit into
the analysis."[11] The facts of romance have disclosed
ideas with possibility of wide significance; and in the
stage of precise progress we acquire other facts in a
systematic order, which thereby form both a disclosure
and an analysis of the general subject matter of romance.[12]

"This stage is the sole stage of learning in the traditional scheme of education, either at school or university." [13] To its being a stage, Whitehead has, of course,
no objection. "There is no getting away from the fact
that things have been found out, and that to be effective in the modern world you must have a store of
definite acquirement of the best practice."[14] His objection merely is that in the traditional scheme discipline is not preceded by the stage of romance, and thus
tends to produce inert knowledge without initiative or
else to arouse contempt for ideas.[15] Furthermore, since
this precision is not followed by adequate generalization, the knowledge remains inert and unutilized.[16]

The third and final stage, that of generalization, is
"a return to romanticism with added advantage of
classified ideas and relevant technique. It is the fruition which has been the goal of the precise training."[17]
"The pupil now wants to use his new weapons. He is an
effective individual, and it is effects he wants to produce."[18] Hence the business of the university is "to
convert the knowledge of a boy into the power of a
man."[19] "The stage of generalization is the stage of
shedding details in favor of the active application of
principles, the details retreating into subconscious
habits. The essence of this stage is the emergence

from the comparative passivity of being trained into the active freedom of application. . . ."[20] Thus the distinctive feature of this stage is application, for this application prevents those ideas gained in the stage of precision from merely lying "inert."

In general these cycles occur in different periods in the student's development. Up to the age of thirteen or fourteen is the romantic stage, fourteen to eighteen the age for precision, and eighteen to twenty-two the age for generalization.[21] But the ages indicated are intended to be only averages and rough approximations,[22] and the phases of different subjects occur at different times. Thus since the child acquires speech in infancy, the stage of romance in language begins very early, to be followed by its stage of precision. As literary experience reaches the stage of precision, the romantic stage of science begins. By the time the stage of precision is reached in science, literary studies are at the stage of generalization.[23] Thus the major cycles are out of phase so as not to compete and conflict with each other;[24] and at no time are the distinctions between the cycles as clear-cut as analysis might make it appear. But there is an alternation of dominance.[25] There are also cycles within cycles,[26] since, as we have seen, "the student must be continually enjoying some fruition and starting afresh."[27] What is wanted is "a harmony of patterns," produced by coordinating the various elements into subordinate cycles, each of intrinsic worth for the immediate apprehension of the student.[28]

The preceding sketch is a very brief résumé of Whitehead's cyclic theory of education; he makes a more detailed application of the general theory to history and other aspects of "intellectual education," to science, to the arts, and to "emotional education" than I have indicated. And two other essays in *The Aims of Education*, "The Place of the Classics in Education" and "The Mathematical Curriculum," are based on similar principles.[29]  But this general outline will suffice for the present.

Probably the most striking parallel with this theory which appears in a later, non-educational work appears in the first chapter of *Modes of Thought*. Here, speaking of philosophic thought in general, Whitehead says that "systematization" is necessary. But he points out that there is a necessary prior stage, that of "assemblage,"[30] and points to John Stuart Mill as one whose mentality "was limited by his peculiar education which gave him system before any enjoyment of the relevant experience."[31] The parallelism of "assemblage" and "systematization" to "romance" and "precision" is obvious, and Whitehead's use of the one pair in an introductory chapter of a later book on general modes of thought would suggest that he saw this general sequence as part of what might be called a "law of learning."

This intrinsically rhythmic and cyclic character of learning stems from the fact that life itself is rhythmic and cyclic: "Wherever there is some rhythm, there is some life."[32] And Whitehead's development of the "Way of Rhythm" on the general cosmological level is very similar to the educational rhythms just sketched.

The Way of Rhythm prevades all life, and indeed all physical existence. This common principle of Rhythm

> is one of the reasons for believing that the root principles
> of life are, in some lowly form, exemplified in all types of
> physical existence. In the Way of Rhythm a round of
> experiences, forming a determinate sequence of contrasts
> attainable within a definite method, are codified so that
> the end of one such cycle is the proper antecedent stage
> for the beginning of another such cycle. The cycle is such
> that its own completion provides the conditions for its
> own mere repetition. It eliminates the fatigue attendant
> upon the repetition of any one of its parts. . . . Provided
> that each cycle in itself is self-repairing, the fatigue from
> repetition requires a high level of coordination of stretches
> of past experience.[33]

Thus far in the preceding quotation, Whitehead has
been speaking of the Way of Rhythm as one of the
ways (along with the Way of Blindness and the Way
of Transience) in which stabilization or a thwarting
of the urge toward novel contrast is secured. Life
simply runs in recurrent cycles. But his discussion
continues in a way more relevant to the rhythm of
education.

> At the level of human experience we do find fatigue
> arising from the mere repetition of cycles. The device
> by which this fatigue is again obviated takes the form
> of the preservation of the fundamental abstract structure
> of the cycle, combined with the variation of the concrete
> details of succeeding cycles. This device is particularly
> illustrated in music and in vision. It is of course capable
> of enormous elaboration of complexity of detail. Thus the
> Rhythm of life is not merely to be sought in simple cyclic
> recurrence. *The cycle element is driven into the founda-*
> *tion, and variations of cycles, and cycles of cycles are*
> *elaborated.*[34]

The education of all organisms then, not merely of human organisms, is rhythmic. "Consider how nature generally sets to work to educate the living organisms which teem on this earth. You cannot begin to understand nature's method unless you grasp the fact that the essential spring of all growth is within you. . . . The regular method of nature is a happy process of general encouragement." [35] "The question is how to introduce the freedom of nature into the orderliness of knowledge." [36] The processes of formal education should correspond to "the rhythmic character of growth." [37] and thus it will satisfy "natural cravings," [38] "the rhythmic cravings of the pupil," [39] "the call of life within the child." [40] That life, growth, and learning are rhythmic are examples, perhaps, of what Whitehead calls "self-evidence" [41] and must perhaps be placed on trial before Whitehead's ultimate court of appeal, "the reaction of our own nature to the general aspect of life in the universe."[42]

Apart from this appeal to general experience, Whitehead would tend to rest his case on the "first natural cycle" which is such a "brilliant success" [43]— in fact, "a miracle." [44] This first cycle of intellectual progress from the baby's achievement of perception to the acquirement of language and on to classified thought and keener perception "is the only cycle of progress which we can observe in its *purely natural* state." [45] Furthermore, though "a new born baby looks like a most unpromising subject for intellectual development when we consider the task before it," this cycle—in contrast to the later educational imitations of it—is a complete success. "At the end of it the child *can* speak, its ideas *are* classified, and its perceptions *are* sharpened." [46] Thus the first, successful, purely natural cycle is taken as the paradigm of all learning.

If progress in mental development is such a natural process and if the completion of one stage produces, more or less automatically, those natural cravings which give rise to the next stage, it is relevant to ask why the school and the teacher should not stand out of the way and let the machinery of nature take over. Since it is easy for a teacher to damage a delicate organism,[47] might there be something to be said for dispensing with him and thus preventing his having an opportunity to do damage? An extreme "naturalistic" view of education would tend to assert this position.

To a considerable degree Whitehead would accept this naturalistic view. "We . . . schoolmasters and . . . . dons are apt to forget that we are only subordinate elements in the education of a grown man; and that in their own good time, in later life our pupils will learn for themselves. The phenomena of growth cannot be hurried beyond certain narrow limits." [48] The possibilities for aiding natural growth are of two sorts. First, education can improve on nature by preventing that waste which is part of nature's method, and by aiding nature in providing a suitable environment and keeping interest alive.[49] Second, the human organism is not exclusively a natural product. "After all the child is the heir to long ages of civilization, and it is absurd to let him wander in the intellectual maze of men in the Glacial Epoch. Accordingly a certain pointing out of important facts, and of sim-

plifying ideas, and of usual names, really strengthens
the natural impetus of the pupil." [50] But even here
the products of civilization are considered primarily as
pedagogical aids to this natural impetus toward knowledge. Whitehead, in his educational writings, has
little to say about the artificial or non-natural elements
which stem from society. They are for his system, of
course, all of one piece with the natural. All constitute the environment which is available as data for
the concrescent organism.

The other important element in Whitehead's views
on pedagogical method is actually already implicit in
his cyclic doctrine—an organic unity which by this
time we should perhaps have come to expect. This
other element is his constant emphasis on movement
from the particular to the general, from the concrete
to the abstract, and then the reverse.[51] "The essential
course of reasoning is to generalize what is particular and then to particularize what is general. Without generality there is no reasoning, without concreteness there is no importance." [52] The same is true with
the theoretical and the practical as we have already
seen. First-hand experience shows the need for theory
and the possibility of it; but theory in turn must find
its application in practice.[53] But all this is inherent
in the cyclic doctrine. The romantic experience at first
hand with the concrete particulars which the student
encounters about him will lead to those few important
ideas, which are general, abstract, and theoretical.
But the stage of generalization gives the student a
chance to use these new weapons, to see their range
of applicability, to produce effects—in short, to return
from the abstract to the concrete.

1. *The Aims of Education*, p. 24.

2. *Ibid.*, p. 25.

3. *Ibid.*, *pp.* 25–26. Cf. "The problem of a curriculum is not so much the succession of subjects, for all subjects should in essence be begun with the dawn of mentality. The truly important order is the order of quality which the educational procedure should assume."—*Ibid.*, p. 44.

4. *Ibid.*, p. 27: "Life is essentially periodic."

5. *Ibid.*, p. 30.

6. *Ibid.*, p. 28.

7. *Ibid.*, p. 50.

8. *Ibid.*, p. 52. This same general view is later advanced in *Science and the Modern World*, p. 285: "The general training should aim at eliciting our concrete apprehensions, and should satisfy the itch of youth to be doing something. There should be some analysis even here, but just enough to illustrate the ways of thinking in diverse spheres." Similarly, "We must grasp the topic in the rough before we smooth it out and shape it."—*Modes of Thought*, p. 8.

9. *Science and the Modern World*, p. 285.

10. *Ibid.*, p. 52. Cf. *The Function of Reason*, p. 17: " . . . The end of one such cycle is the proper antecedent stage for the beginning of another such cycle."

11. *The Aims of Education*, p. 29.

12. *Ibid.*, p. 29.

13. *Ibid.*, p. 53.

14. *Ibid.*, p. 53.

15. *Ibid.*, p. 52.

16. *Ibid.*, p. 50.

17. *Ibid.*, p. 30.

18. *Ibid.*, p. 57.

19. *Ibid.*, p. 43.

20. *Ibid.*, p. 58.

21. *Ibid.*, p. 59.

22. *Ibid.*, p. 59. So in another essay, he speaks of sixteen (rather than eighteen) as the age at which the student is rapidly maturing and at which the student's "keen delight in generalizations" is seen as ushering in this phase of education in science (*Essays in Science and Philosophy*, p. 146).

23. *The Aims of Education*, pp. 29–37.

24. *Ibid.*, p. 33.

25. *Ibid.*, p. 44.

26. *Ibid.*, p. 60.   Cf. *The Function of Reason*, p. 17.

27. *The Aims of Education*, p. 30.

28. *Ibid.*, p. 33.

29. These two essays are treated in the next chapter, "The Curriculum." The other educational writings do not make much of the terms "romance," "precision," and "generalization," but the same principles seem to be involved. So, for example, "Science in General Education" contains a discussion of the "soft" and "hard" elements in the scientific curriculum. Part of the soft element consists of "browsing in the laboratory, the observatory, or in the field—anything the student does for himself according to his own fancy." The other part of the soft element consists of general lectures to excite interest in the various sciences. The "hard" element, on the other hand, consists of the "attainment of exact knowledge based on first-hand observation with the concepts and generalizations illustrated and tested by practical work" (*Essays in Science and Philosophy*, pp. 144-46). The resemblance of the "soft element" to "romance" and of the "hard element" to "precision" is clear. But I do not find in this essay any mention of a rhythmic or sequential relation of these two elements. They seem to run concurrently in this stage of general education, the "pre-sixteen" period. But then a period of generalization does follow (*Essays in Science and Philosophy*, p. 146).

30. *Modes of Thought*, p. 2.

31. *Ibid.*, p. 8.

32. *An Enquiry Concerning the Principles of Natural Knowledge* (2nd ed.; Cambridge: Cambridge University Press, 1955), p. 197.

33. *The Function of Reason*, pp. 16–17.

34. *Ibid.*, p. 17 (italics added).

35. *Essays in Science and Philosophy*, p. 126.

36. *Ibid.*, p. 160.

37. *The Aims of Education*, p. 43.

38. *Ibid.*, p. 50.

39. *Ibid.*, p. 31.

40. *Ibid.*, p. 51.

41. *Modes of Thought*, pp. 66–67.

42. *Essays in Science and Philosophy*, p. 72.

43. *The Aims of Education*, p. 32.

44. *Ibid.*, pp. 25–26.

45. *Ibid.*, p. 31 (italics added).

46. *Ibid.*, p. 31 (italics Whitehead's).

47. *Ibid.*, p. 53; *Essays in Science and Philosophy*, p. 145.

48. *The Aims of Education*, p. 53.

49. *Ibid.*, p. 62.

50. *Ibid.*, pp. 51–52.

51. E.g., *ibid.*, pp. 97, 111, 121; *Science and the Modern World*, p. 284; *Essays in Science and Philosophy*, pp. 26, 142–43, 151.

52. *The Aims of Education*, pp. 82–83.

53. Cf. also, "Firsthand knowledge is the ultimate basis of intellectual life. To a large extent book-learning conveys second-hand information, and as such can never give rise to the importance of immediate practice."—*Ibid.*, p. 79.

# XI.  The Curriculum

WHITEHEAD does not have the air of a man undertaking fundamental curriculum reform.  He framed many of his remarks in relation to the three general types of curriculums familiar to his British audiences: the literary or liberal curriculum, the scientific, and the technical.  But this apparent limitation to traditional curriculums is somewhat deceptive.  These three merely constitute what may be called the "raw stuff" for Whitehead's proposed curriculum, not solid units in his new structure.  Moreover, he felt free to add elements which were not in the British tradition but which he felt were necessary components of the new whole he wished to produce.  In short his ultimate curriculum is a synthesis not so limited by tradition as might appear.

We have already seen an attempt at synthesis in his remarks in regard to general and specialized education in his discussion of the ends of education.  There he began with the familiar distinction between these two types of education and their associated curriculums.  But the distinction, insofar as it is based on the nature or number of the subjects studied, is soon destroyed.  "There is not one course of study which merely gives

general culture and another which gives special knowledge. . . . You may not divide the seamless cloak of
learning."[1]  "There is only one subject-matter for education and that is Life in all its manifestations."[2]
Hence we must make every effort to avoid what Whitehead calls the "fatal disconnection" between subjects.

It might seem as if the distinction between liberal
and specialized education could be preserved on the
basis of how a given subject is treated.[3]  But even this
separation is partial since each mode of treatment is
closely connected with the other and gives rise to it.
"The subjects pursued for the sake of general education are special subjects specially studied; and on the
other hand, one of the ways of encouraging mental
activity is to foster a special devotion."[4]  Not merely
is the distinction based on subject matter and mode
of treatment evanescent, but, as we have seen, the
apparently distinct kinds of outcome (understanding
and power) toward which the two curricula are pointed
also blend and become unified in wisdom.

The specific manner in which a synthesis is to be
achieved between the three traditional curriculums
(literary, scientific, and technical) is as follows. Starting with the liberal or literary education, Whitehead
calls it a very good education for certain people whose
type of mind it fits.  It was intended for a leisured,
governing class, and for them it did very well.[5] But
the traditional liberal education had several severe
limitations.  "The expression of the human spirit is
not confined to literature.  There are the other arts,
and there are the sciences.  Also education must pass
beyond the passive reception of the ideas of others."[6]
Third, as Whitehead points out in his "Autobiographi-

cal Notes," his own education, which was in the older literary tradition and of which he thinks Plato would have approved, "was very limited in its application to life."[7]  Fourth, "In the area of logic, ancient thought is useless in working with the application of logical ideas to practice; here only the examination of the methods of science can give what is required."[8]  And this lack of utility in practice is only part of a fifth and larger charge to be brought against the Platonic education:  "The insistence in the Platonic culture on disinterested intellectual appreciation is a psychological error. . . . Essentially culture should be for action."[9]  As we have seen, one way of stating the aim of education is the "marriage of thought and action."[10] And finally, "An evil side of the Platonic culture has been its total neglect of technical education as an ingredient in the complete development of ideal human beings. This neglect has arisen from two disastrous antitheses, namely, that between mind and body, and that between thought and action."[11]  In sum, then, though the literary education had its values, science must be added[12] and technical training, too, must make its contribution.  The inference seems quite clear, then, that it is developments in political and economic democracy, in technology, and in the fields of knowledge generally which bring Whitehead to this position; and the result which he seeks is possibly best summed up in his statement: "In the democracy of the future every man and every woman will be trained for a free intellectual life by an education which is directly related to their immediate lives as citizens and as workers, and thereby elicits speculations and curiosities and hopes which range through the whole universe."[13]

The preceding list of six shortcomings of the traditional liberal education indicates why Whitehead seeks
to synthesize the liberal curriculum with the scientific
and the technical. Nor are the various elements anti-
thetical, in his opinion. He denies any fundamental
separation: "There can be no adequate technical education which is not liberal, and no liberal education
which is not technical."[14] Likewise Whitehead believes
that a less faulty view of education would reduce the
antagonism which we feel exists between the claims of
pure knowledge and specialized acquirement.[15] What
Whitehead seeks, then, is a synthesis such that each of
these curriculums should include the other two and
that each should be illuminated by the others.[16]

These three curriculums (or elements of them) are,
however, not to be tossed together into a potpourri
or glued together into some kind of jerrybuilt structure. "A mere mechanical mixture of the three curricula will produce bad results in the shape of scraps
of information never interconnected or utilized."[17]
This mixture would actually produce those "inert
ideas" which Whitehead was trying so hard to avoid.
He continues: "We have already noted as one of the
strong points of the traditional literary culture that
all its parts are coordinated. The problem of education
is . . . without loss of coordination to infuse into each
way of education something of the other two."[18]

But the expansions in Whitehead's proposed curriculum do not stop merely with conflation of three traditional ones. Some additional elements not appearing
in any of them are to become part of the synthesis. One
such addition is the greater emphasis on the arts, par-

ticularly the fine arts.[19]  But we must be careful to
note that, as a term, "art" appears equivocal since it is
subjected to dialectical treatment.  Thus we could
properly conclude that the introduction of art into the
curriculum at one level might mean little more than a
traditional art course and its traditional contents.  But
its function and purpose is more than that.  We have,
for example, already seen the function of art as giving
that vision which is necessary for control and direction,[20] a function which might be classified as "art"
at a middle dialectical level.  At a higher level, art for
Whitehead is any process of selection by which the
concrete facts are so arranged as to elicit attention to
the concrete values which are realizable by them.[21]
These concrete facts, the individualized parts, are
individualized values.  Thus art is the habit of appre-
hending such facts, parts, or organisms in their
completeness, of enjoying these vivid values, of appre-
hending what lies beyond oneself. Getting into position
to view a sunset is an elementary form of art; understanding a modern factory in all its ramifications is
another form.

The purpose behind the development of all such
habits of aesthetic appreciation is to increase the depth
of individuality.[22]  The organism is what it prehends,
and its uniqueness, its individuality, is a function of
the uniqueness of the pattern by which it prehends a
wide range of data.  The more limited the range of
data on which it can draw, the shallower its individuality.  Increase in this range is a necessary preliminary for its depth in individuality.  In short, art, as
imparting this sensitivity over a wide range, is a neces-

sary condition for the creative novelty toward which
the organism and the universe are to advance and is,
in fact, the major justification for broadening the curriculum by combining the traditional three as Whitehead suggests.

How fundamental the concept of art is for Whitehead we saw earlier in his definition of civilization:
a civilized society is one which exhibits the qualities of
Truth, Beauty, Adventure, Art, and Peace.[23]  There
is also what may be called a pedagogical function of
art, at several of these contextual levels.  Thus Whitehead states:

> Every subject of study should be presented as in the ab-
> stract and in the concrete. Both sides are wanted. We
> learn them in the abstract, we feel them in the concrete.
> . . . The function of art is to turn the abstract into the
> concrete and the concrete into the abstract.[24]

The essentially aesthetic quality of Whitehead's system
and the part in it played by art indicate quite clearly
that he would enormously expand the role of art (in
all these senses) in education.

Whitehead would wish to add also a religious element to the curriculum.[25]  But we have already seen in
Whitehead's discussion of the aims of education enough
of his sense of "religious" to realize that he does not
intend by it mere instruction in dogma or doctrine.  On
the other hand, the sense of "religious" in that discussion [26] is not the only sense of the word for Whitehead
as can be seen from the development given it in *Religion in the Making*. Certain obvious similarities stand
out clearly, however.  "A religion, on its doctrinal side,

can thus be defined as a system of *general truths* which have the effect of transforming character when they are sincerely held and vividly apprehended."[27]   But discussion of what exactly is implied by "religion" seems best postponed for a moment until we can discuss it in connection with "importance."

As we attempt to see what Whitehead's synthesis might involve, several rather obvious preliminary problems demand attention prior to any specific effort to state the synthesis.  Possibly the most crass of these is the problem of lack of time.

Even if one grants that the aims and materials of the three curricula are compatible, a synthesis of them would necessarily involve some drastic curtailment in each.  Three curricula plus some additions must now occupy the space formerly taken by one.

Few writers on education are as well aware of the problems inherent in the shortness of time as is Whitehead.  He refers to it almost continually [28] and speaks of it as "the rock on which the fairest educational schemes are wrecked." [29]  Whitehead is well aware that the period demanded by his new curriculum must be no longer than that of the older ones.  Compression or omission must occur.

Omission is secured in several different ways.  First, we must realize that "no human being can attain to anything but fragmentary knowledge and a fragmentary training of his capacities." [30]  "We must take it as an unavoidable fact, that God has so made the world that there are more topics desirable for knowledge than any one person can possibly acquire. It is hopeless to approach the problem by way of the enumeration of subjects which every one ought to have mastered. There are too many of them, all with excellent title-deeds." [31] The synthesis will not attempt, then, those familiar goals: to include everything that the educated man should know or even perhaps a full development of the individual's capacities. The result will at best be a fragment. The problem of how this fragment is to be selected still remains.

Some elimination will occur on the basis of effectiveness. Whitehead knows that it is not enough to assert that a subject is valuable in that it produces certain educational consequences. The educator must consider whether this same value might not be obtained more quickly and easily through some other subject or combination of subjects.[32] Thus once the content of education is selected provisionally, purely pragmatic considerations of pedagogical effectiveness will suggest the elimination of certain subjects. But this result will occur only in so far as a given subject is a less efficient means for all pupils. For the moment we may leave open the question whether such an educational generalization is possible.

A third means of reducing the bulk, the major one for Whitehead, consists of avoiding needless details and cutting out the deadwood now in the three curriculums. After the most anxious inquiry, the teacher will select what is essential, avoiding "a lot of irrelevant stuff of inferior importance." [33] Only such selection will produce that "certain ruthless definiteness" which is essential to education [34] and will make possible "the simple study of a few general truths, well illustrated by practical examples." [35] In short, the material of inferior importance will be pruned out and the emphasis will be on "the general ideas used, and their possibilities of importance when subjected to further study." [36]

If we take "importance" in this quotation in its usual senses, Whitehead is uttering merely an educational platitude. Everyone who has ever had anything to do with education has favored pruning out the deadwood. Unfortunately, importance in these usual senses does not take us far as a criterion for elimination. No teacher wittingly teaches a lot of inferior or irrelevant stuff. Everyone believes that everything which he teaches is important in some sense: important for the trained chemist to know, important for a sound knowledge of chemistry, and the like.

If Whitehead makes any contribution to the problem, it lies in the sense in which he uses "importance." And this sense, it seems fairly clear, is the sense in which he uses it in his cosmological works. For example, as early as the essays in *The Aims of Education* we find the statement:

> The ultimate motive power, alike in science, in morality and in religion, is the sense of value, the sense of importance. It takes the various forms of wonder of curiosity, of reverence, of worship, of tumultous desire for merging personality in something beyond itself.[37]

This, obviously, is that same importance which we met in the cosmological works, that aspect of the expression of the actual entity which emphasizes its linkage with the rest of the cosmos. Importance in this sense must, then, mean something more than mere parochial significance for the individual student or for the particular body of knowledge.

In any case, the problem of unifying the literary, scientific, and technological curriculums will not be solved by a single course of study for all students. First of all, each student will select some area of specialization according to his natural bent and his capacities. This will be that "something he knows well." [38] "The watchword must be 'concentration.' " [39] With the other areas of knowledge he will have a much more superficial acquaintance. But, like a good Platonist, Whitehead hopes that acquaintance through the "leading truths" and "general ideas" will help produce understanding and wisdom in these other areas too.

This solution to the problem is familiar, and it entails two equally familiar problems. The first is the extent to which emphasis on "leading truths" can actually produce a saving of time. Whitehead is well aware that general principles and main ideas cannot be meaningful or useful apart from the particulars from which they developed and which they organize and describe. Unless generalizations are taught as derived from some body of data and applicable to it, they are vacuous, "empty sounds." [40] We have seen enough of Whitehead's distrust of inert ideas and his emphasis on romance and application to know that Whitehead's program is not to be a concatenation of generalizations. The importance of application is, in fact, a primary reason for the inclusion of technical education in his curricular synthesis. "There is no royal road to learning through an airy path of brilliant generalizations." "All practical teachers know that education is the patient process of the mastery of details, minute by minute, hour by hour, day by day." [41] But obviously the more that generalizations must be supported and applied, the less time will be left for the generalizations themselves, i.e., the fewer the generalizations which can be well taught. Whitehead obviously feels that a relatively few generalizations will do the job, but whether his estimate is realistic or not is another matter.

The second problem connected with this sort of solution is whether it implies a different kind of experience in each subject for the specialist in it as opposed to the non-specialist. For the general student, the emphasis can be on the leading ideas, with only enough supporting detail to make them meaningful and applicable. But specialized knowledge tends to be detailed knowledge. And the traditional course in most subjects has, consequently, carried a mass of detail because it was intended to afford a firm grounding for the future specialist. Thus the general education movement in this country has tended to develop parallel courses for specialists and non-specialists, on the grounds that the course of study for the non-specialist should be qualitatively as well as quantitatively different from the work offered the specialist.

Whitehead everywhere adopts the solution of this problem which rests on a chronological differentiation between the two types of education. Possibly he does so only because he sees this as the solution which had been generally adopted in Britain at the time he wrote.[42] At any rate, this is the framework Whitehead consistently adopts. Education up to about sixteen or seventeen is to be general, and the demands of specialization must yield. Students will share a similar general education, and only the additional courses will be specialized.[43] This program would mean that the specialized fields would have to meet some demands they have historically been unwilling to meet. For example, in the mathematics program which Whitehead sketches for general education, the amount of trigonometry is sharply reduced.[44] This selection means that the student later specializing in mathematics will have to take additional trigonometry in order to acquire those parts necessary for specialization in mathematics but not necessary for general education. By and large, teachers of mathematics (and the same is true of teachers in other areas) have been loath to accept this sort of solution. Their feeling has been that the "well-prepared" student came to specialization in mathematics with an "adequate" knowledge of trigonometry; if this course involves too much detail for the general student, so much the worse for the general student. Whitehead clearly is not prepared to accept this latter view and apparently believes that specialization will not suffer from the kind of elimination of detail which he suggests.

But even if we accept this solution, difficulties remain. Whitehead's suggestions all tend to expand the curriculum (e.g., the addition of technical elements to the liberal and scientific curriculums, the introduction of shopwork as the application of geometry, and more "art" and "religion"). And he does so in spite of his clear recognition of the immense difficulties caused by the relative lack of time. Yet the chief device which he emphasizes for overcoming this problem is to simplify the details but emphasize the important principles and applications.[45]

The curriculum, particularly that of the American high school and college, has been under a pressure of expansion such as Whitehead probably never dreamed of at the time he wrote about the English school. A host of "subjects"—consumer education, citizenship education, driver education, safety education, "careers," to name only a few while omitting those more exotic additions such as baton twirling, cosmetology, or fly-casting, so often cited by the critics of modern education—press for a place in the curriculum. Possibly if Whitehead had had the problem in the contemporary American context, he too would have felt the need for additional principles of exclusion.

If we try to determine more specifically what a synthesis which combines these three curriculums would contain, we can get a fairly full answer by joining Whitehead's remarks on this connection to his rhythmic or cyclic theory. It would seem that such a weaving together of his comments is not merely possible but even intended by him. Such difficulties as arise do not stem from conflicts among his statements. Where he is explicit, he seems consistent. Rather the problems concern points about which it is uncertain what precise disposition Whitehead wished to make of them. By and large then, an examination of his major educational cycles yields a fairly precise curricular plan which does achieve the integration of the literary, the scientific, and the technical curriculums.

In his discussions of rhythm, Whitehead stresses two cycles, a linguistic-literary one and a scientific-mathematical, which are easily related to the liberal and scientific curricula. The first part of the linguistic cycle consists of a minor cycle (with its own phases of romance, precision, and generalization) in which the child masters his native language. This part of the cycle is the most difficult; but, as Whitehead says, it is successful (which is more than can be said for some of the others) and should serve as the general paradigm for the later, more artificial cycles of formal education.[46] Another period of romance begins in this cycle with adolescence. Whitehead's statements about its contents are very, very general. He speaks of it simply as involving acquaintance with artistry in words, sounds, and colors.[47] This program bespeaks a rather extended curriculum at the early elementary-school level in literature, art, and music. But Whitehead nowhere goes into detail on these matters. Nor does he in regard to the "eddies" of precision which appear in this dominantly romantic phase of the cycle; he leaves the discussion at the level of "the perfection of writing, of spelling, of the elements of arithmetic, and of lists of simple facts, such as the kings of England."[48] The development of an actual curriculum for these school years would demand considerable filling in of Whitehead's sketch.

The elements involved in the following major stage of adolescent precision are: a command of English, the ability to read simple French fluently, a knowledge of elementary Latin, and, for the more gifted students, an introduction to Greek.[49] This stage would also involve the treatment of the semi-literary subjects such as history through the study of the languages and literatures. At the close of this period, the stage of generalization in the linguistic-literary cycle would involve the reading of literature and the general history in which it is imbedded, to be followed by a period of precision in history through the intensive study of a short definite period of history.[50] Here again, some things in these stages of precision and generalization Whitehead has sketched with considerable precision. So, for example, he has outlined a possible classical curriculum in some detail and has suggested the kind of procedures and outcomes which the study of history through work with languages and literatures would entail. Other matters do not receive much development beyond the statements paraphrased above.

In one important respect, his treatment of the linguistic-literary cycle differs from that given the scientific-mathematical one. In his discussion of the classical curriculum he explicitly states that he does not believe that the route through the classical languages is the *sole* road to the ends he seeks for the student. He rests his case for the classical languages in preference to other studies simply on the grounds that, at the time he spoke, this program did fit the majority of pupils, had the strongest tradition, and was most easily manageable by the existing corps of teachers.[51] Quite clearly, then, changed conditions in these regards would suggest the achievement by students of the same objectives through the study of other languages or other material. There is not the same note of necessity for using classical languages here as that which, as we shall see, attends his discussion of parts of the scientific-mathematical cycle.

The objectives for the study of the classical languages are stated very generally: "To develop the mind in the regions of logic, philosophy, history, and of aesthetic apprehension of literary beauty."[52] More specifically this experience involves the analysis of the Latin sentence as a particular and concrete example of logical analysis, the study of Greek and Roman history as specific and important examples of historical periods, and accquaintance with the two literatures as affording both models of literary excellence and examples of personalities which exhibit greatness on a grand scale (whether for good or ill).

From the nature of these more specific objectives, it is once more apparent how "dispensable" are the classical languages in the curriculum. Their function is largely exemplary; and other languages, other literatures, and other periods of history could probably furnish equally suitable concrete examples of a similar sort. Similarity, in art, history, and religion, Whitehead would probably always see as possible a multiplicity of routes toward the general objectives and would allow the specific kind of experience or material to be chosen on the basis of rather temporary or local criteria, as he did in making his case for the classical languages.

When we come to the other cycle that he discusses, the scientific-mathematical one, we find more detail. This statement is particularly true of the mathematical part. As a mathematician, Whitehead doubtlessly felt greatest interest and competence in this part of the curriculum. Likewise, as a famous scholar in this field, he was given several opportunities to speak his mind on mathematical education. As a result, we have two essays and a number of passing comments which develop his thoughts on mathematical training as far as general education is concerned.

As we should expect, Whitehead again stresses throughout those "few general ideas of far-reaching importance."[53] "those of quantity and of space, which are of fundamental importance."[54] And once more

there is Whitehead's acknowledgment that education
cannot begin with these general ideas but must lead toward them by starting with particulars and simple illustrations of these ideas.[55]   But again we meet his
reiteration that work with these examples is only a
pointless accumulation of details unless these are seen
as direct illustrations of these main ideas.[56]

The aims of the work in mathematics are also consonant with the general aims we saw stated earlier.
General ideas in mathematics are abstract, but one important reason for including mathematics within the
curriculum of general education is to train the student
in handling abstract ideas.[57]   There is also a second
reason: Mathematics "is the chief instrument for discipline in logical method."[58]   But this latter involves
more than a mere knowledge of the valid types of reasoning and some practice which enables one to follow
them.  "The art of reasoning consists in getting hold
of the subject at the right end, and of seizing on the
few general ideas which illuminate the whole, and of
persistently marshalling all subsidiary facts around
them."[59]  Thus this second reason for teaching mathematics also involves abstract ideas and the relating of
them to their relevant particulars.  Hence Whitehead
can say of the mathematical curriculum as a whole:
"The goal to be aimed at is that the pupil should
acquire familiarity with abstract thought, should realize how it applies to particular concrete circumstances,
and should know how to apply general methods to its
logical investigation."[60]

The content of the course would be roughly as follows. In childhood, in the stage of romance, the student
has encountered certain mathematical ideas; though

this stage is dominated by romance, it has its elements of precision, among which is the strengthening of the elementary arithmetical processes.[61] In adolescence these arithmetical abilities are strengthened, and the student acquires the elements of algebra and geometry and gains some experience in applying this knowledge to the problems of surveying and other scientific work involving calculation.[62] Now a year's work in science "should make everyone understand the main principles which govern the development of mechanics, physics, chemistry, algebra, and geometry."[63] As far as algebra and geometry are concerned, we see what these main ideas are as Whitehead lists them for the final review at the end of the general course: the fundamental properties of quantity which lead to physical measurement, functionality (particularly as involved in the precise expression of physical laws and in historical and sociological statistics), and the history of mathematics as illuminative of the general development of mathematical thought. The part dealing with geometry, "the queen of the physical sciences,"[64] would treat congruence, similarity, a limited amount of trigonometry, analytic geometry, and projective geometry.[65] This program is offered as an ideal, and Whitehead admits that ideals are never fully realized. Nevertheless he insists that, as sketched, it is of workable compass. To this, one can say only that this course is of far greater rigor and extent than most general education programs in this country have ever managed to achieve.

The principle of selection operating in the development of this curriculum is that these materials are the ones which make possible the achievement of those major contributions earlier attributed to the study of mathematics: familiarity with abstract ideas and skill in handling them, knowledge of their applications, and ability to treat them logically. Because mathematics has this close relation to modern logical thought (knowledge of which Whitehead believes is almost indispensable[66]) and to science (which seems equally indispensable in coping with the modern world[67]) mathematics appears to him a necessary part of the curriculum. The only problem is to make it effective by including as many relevant major principles and their applications as possible and by excluding those details which lead nowhere. Shopwork, science, and technology provide ample opportunity for application. In fact, as Whitehead makes out the case for mathematics, it comes very close to being a subject (provided the materials are properly selected) which is educational in itself—Whitehead's dictum that there are no such subjects notwithstanding. We do not, therefore, get any light on what might serve as a principle of exclusion for subjects of less basic importance in understanding the modern world.

The other, or science, part of the mathematical-scientific cycle, Whitehead sketches in less detail. Its stage of romance would consist of the browsing involved in chemical experiments, in field trips and collections in geology, zoology, and botany, or in astronomical observations with a small telescope.[68] The hard core of the stage of precision would necessarily be confined to one or two sciences.[69] Whitehead's examples—and probably his preferences—are physics and chemistry. The other sciences could not be subjects for serious study at the level of general education level simply because of the lack of time. Consequently, the leading ideas or general principles of physiology, botany, astronomy, geology, and the rest (or physics and chemistry if two sciences other than these were the ones chosen for major attention) would have to be imparted through a series of lectures.[70] Whitehead has no illusions about the efficacy of the lecture method, but no other procedure seems possible in view of the lack of time.

The precision thus gained in regard to science would receive its application, not merely in its own details, but also in technical subjects. One form of this same principle is the necessity that technical education find the science or sciences underlying a given technology and show how they are in fact applied in the technology.[71]

Having glanced at such details as Whitehead gives us, if we move to larger questions of curriculum structure, two familiar problems concern the horizontal and vertical organization, i.e., the relations between various educational experiences which the student has concurrently, on the one hand, and the basis for ordering them sequentially, on the other. Whitehead's rhythmic principle gives partial guidance in regard to both.

Whitehead emphasizes the importance of the horizontal organization or, as he calls it, "the coordination of studies" or "the way in which the different tasks set . . . play into each other's hands." In fact he believes that the rate of the student's progress can be doubled if proper co-ordination of studies is achieved. It is the attempt to produce this sort of co-ordination which leads him to his synthesis of the three curriculums, for it is in the proper use of application that he sees much of this efficiency gained. For example, the application of mathematics and science to shopwork makes the principles of the former less inert and illumines the activities of the latter. In regard to the vertical organization, also, his doctrine of rhythm makes several points quite clear. The linguistic cycle is the first one because this is the one with which the child starts in nature. Second, the other cycles must be kept out of phase with it and with one another in order to avoid mutual interference. Thus, when language has reached a stage of precision, some other cycle can begin the stage of romance.

But this principle, if taken strictly, allows room for only three cycles "or subjects" at a given time. If the student were to study more than three areas at a given time, then there would be duplication of the stages. But three cycles seem ample room for the content as he seems to envisage it, even if mathematics and science are each given separate cycles; for the technical curriculum would probably find its place in the application and generalization phases of the cycles given to the other curriculums. There is, however, the practical problem that these cycles individually will not move with the periodicity of a clockwork. Some phases of some cycles will continue longer than the originally contemporary phase of some other cycle and keeping the cycles out of phase, even in only three subject areas, will demand feats of curriculum engineering. And when we come, as we must, to the cycles within cycles, the complications become truly enormous. There is also the additional difficulty that much of secondary and higher education involves predominantly the stage of precision, with romance and generalization constituting at best occasional eddies in the general cycle. Whitehead would hope that the fact that adequate romance had somewhere preceded would make this precision as endurable and meaningful to the student as possible.

In concluding this survey of Whitehead's views on the curriculum, the significant point to be made is that his more specific goals for parts of the curriculum and the criteria which he develops from them for the selection of materials are essentially those which he stated explicitly in his discussion of the aims of education and implicitly in his cosmological works. There is the same emphasis on the disinterested understanding of the world through a grasp of the major principles which organize and clarify experience, on the ability to utilize ideas and improve the world through the application of scientific and technological power, on sensitivity to beauty and harmony of pattern, and on that religious awareness of a cosmos which stretches as background behind and beyond immediate experience.

But thus far we have minimized an important principle of curricular choice. We have seen one aspect: Certain aims are important because this is the way the world is and hence must be dealt with, whether theoretically or practically. But the same points can be made within the frame of another set of terms. Educational experiences are to be selected because of the particular impress which they make upon the student in terms of habit. This, Whitehead says explicitly, is not the view that education has primarily the role of enforcing discipline, mental and physical,[72] nor yet the view of the curriculum as a kind of whetstone which sharpens the mind.[73] Rather

> every training impresses on its recipient a certain character; and the various elements in general education must be so handled as to enrich the final character of the pupil by their contribution. . . . I repeat that primarily this acquirement is not an access of knowledge but a modification of character by the impress of habit.[74]

Whitehead makes this same point again, perhaps even more forcibly, when he connects habits with another major term which we have seen him repeatedly emphasize, "principles." "When I speak of principles I am hardly even thinking of verbal formulations. A principle which has thoroughly soaked into you is rather a mental habit than a formal statement."[75] And if we recall that he is on this same page using "principles" in the same sense as he uses "main ideas" and "leading truths,"[76] we see that the curricular point to which he has given most attention—the stress on general truth and main ideas—is fundamentally a matter of habit. If "mental cultivation is nothing else than the satisfactory way in which the mind functions when it is poked up into activity,"[77] this functioning is habitual and the ideas are not "inert" because they can be so poked up.

Thus as we moved from the aims of education to the curriculum which was to achieve them, so we now turn from the program to the student, on whom these habits are to be impressed.

1. *The Aims of Education*, p. 18.
2. *Ibid.*, p. 10.
3. *Essays in Science and Philosophy*, p. 127.
4. *The Aims of Education*, p. 18. It is in this context that Whitehead's remark about the relative motivation for general and specialized education is to be understood (*ibid.*, pp. 17–18).

5. *Ibid.*, pp. 70–71.

6. *Ibid.*, p. 72.

7. *Essays in Science and Philosophy*, p. 10.

8. *Ibid.*, p. 132.

9. *The Aims of Education*, p. 73.

10. *Essays in Science and Philosophy*, p. 127.

11. *The Aims of Education*, pp. 77–78. Cf. *Essays in Science and Philosophy*, p. 121: "A training in handicraft of all types should form a large element of every curriculum. Education is not merely an appeal to the abstract intelligence. Purposeful activity, intellectual activity, and the immediate sense of worthwhile achievement, should be conjoined in a unity of experience."

12. *Essays in Science and Philosophy*, p. 132: ". . . The astounding success of modern science in transforming the world makes an examination of the elements of its logical methods so vital a part of education."

13. *Ibid.*, p. 127. Or as Whitehead expresses it when discussing technical education: "Give them alert minds exercised in observation and in reasoning with some knowledge of the world about them, and with feeling for beauty. Then a sound training in handicraft will be accompanied with a power of adaptation and a natural love of efficiency. This is the way to produce a happy people of high capacity for production."— *Ibid.*, p. 125.

14. *The Aims of Education*, p. 74.

15. *Ibid.*, p. 43.

16. *Ibid.*, p. 75.

17. *Ibid.*, pp. 84–85.

18. *Ibid.*, p. 85.

19. *Ibid.*, pp. 64, 90–91.

20. *Ibid.*, p. 91. This point was discussed in the section on aims in connection with "duty."

21. Thus he can speak of "art" as "successfully directed attention" (*ibid.*, p. 74).

22. *Science and the Modern World*, pp. 286–88.

23. *Adventures of Ideas*, pp. 353 ff.

24. *Essays in Science and Philosophy*, p. 151.

25. *The Aims of Education*, p. 61.

26. *Ibid.*, p. 23.

27. *Religion in the Making*, p. 15 (italics added).

28. For example, *The Aims of Education*, pp. 75, 84, 94, 96, 109, 129; *Essays in Science and Philosophy*, pp. 134, 141, 147.

29. *Essays in Science and Philosophy*, p. 131.

30. *The Aims of Education*, p. 84. Cf. also *ibid.*, pp. 73–75.

31. *Ibid.*, p. 46. Cf. also *ibid.*, p. 73. On the other hand, Whitehead himself falls into this manner of speaking. In discussing some of the previous failures of general education, he says: "Accordingly every subject in the preliminary training must be so conceived and shaped as yielding, during that period, general aptitudes, general ideas, and knowledge of special facts, which, taken in conjunction, *form a body of acquirement essential to educated people.*"—*Essays in Science and Philosophy*, p. 142 (italics added).

32. *The Aims of Education*, p. 96; *Essays in Science and Philosophy*, p. 142.

33. *The Aims of Education*, pp. 56–57. Cf. the "rigorous process of selection and adaptation" urged for the mathematical curriculum (*ibid.*, p. 119).

34. *Ibid.*, p. 57.

35. *Ibid.*, p. 122.

36. *Ibid.*, p. 123.

37. *Ibid.*, pp. 62–63.

38. *Ibid.*, p. 74.

39. *Essays in Science and Philosophy*, p. 131.

40. *Ibid.*, p. 131. Cf. also *ibid.*, p. 142.

41. *The Aims of Education*, p. 10. ". . . Nine-tenths of the student's time is, and must be, occupied in the apprehension of a succession of details." *Essays in Science and Philosophy*, p. 140. Cf. also *The Aims of Education*, p. 15.

42. *Essays in Science and Philosophy*, p. 141. Cf. also *The Aims of Education*, p. 17.

43. For example, *The Aims of Education*, pp. 17, 122; *Essays in Science and Philosophy*, pp. 133, 141–42.

44. *The Aims of Education*, pp. 130–31; *Essays in Science and Philosophy*, pp. 134–35.

45. *Essays in Science and Philosophy*, p. 139. See also *The Aims of Education*, p. 126.

46. *The Aims of Education*, p. 32.

47. *Ibid.*, p. 34.

48. *Ibid.*, p. 35.

49. *Ibid.*, p. 36.

50. *Ibid.*, p. 38.

51. *Ibid.*, pp. 96–103.

52. *Ibid.*, p. 96.

53. *Ibid.*, p. 119.

54. *Ibid.*, p. 120.

55. *Essays in Science and Philosophy*, p. 135.

56. *The Aims of Education*, pp., 121–22. The viewpoint of the essay "Mathematics and Liberal Education" is the same. There he pleads that the elementary stages of the subject should never become mere "uninteresting prolegomena" to the more advanced parts—parts which the majority of the pupils will never reach (*Essays in Science and Philosophy*, p. 133).

57. *The Aims of Education*, p. 121.

58. *Ibid.*, p. 127.

59. *Ibid.*, p. 128.

60. *Ibid.*, p. 120. The same points are made in the later essay where the purposes of the elementary mathematics course are seen as (1) to leave the pupil with a precise perception of the nature of abstractions, (2) to exemplify the logical treatment of such ideas, and (3) to make familiar the application of these ideas (*Essays in Science and Philosophy*, p. 133).

61. *The Aims of Education*, p. 35.

62. *Ibid.*, p. 38.

63. *Ibid.*, p. 38.

64. *Essays in Science and Philosophy*, p. 138.

65. *The Aims of Education*, pp. 129–34.

66. *Ibid.*, pp. 127, 163 ff.; *Essays in Science and Philosophy*, p. 133.

67. *The Aims of Education*, pp. 22–23, 154–55; *Essays in Science and Philosophy*, pp. 123–25, 128, 130–33, 144.

68. *Essays in Science and Philosophy*, 145.

69. *Ibid.*, p. 144; *The Aims of Education*, pp. 76, 81.

70. *Essays in Science and Philosophy*, pp. 144, 146.

71. *The Aims of Education,* p. 87.

72. *Essays in Science and Philosophy,* p. 140.

73. *The Aims of Education,* pp. 8–9.

74. *Essays in Science and Philosophy,* p. 143.

75. *The Aims of Education,* p. 42.

76. "The really useful training yields a comprehension of a few general principles with a thorough grounding in the way they apply to a variety of concrete details."—*Ibid.,* p. 42.

77. *Ibid.,* p. 42.

## XII. Students and Teachers in the Educational Milieu

DESPITE THE IMPORTANCE of aims, methods, and curriculums, the process of education actually goes on within the student, with this process affected (we hope, aided) by teachers and the total institutional and social context within which it takes place. When we consider education from the viewpoint of the student, we have arrived at that perspective most congenial to Whitehead's cosmological theory.

The student is engaged in a process of self-development, which is more than merely analogous to the general process of concrescence described in the cosmological works. The purpose of education is to stimulate and guide this self-development[1] in accordance with "the general law of rhythmic progress in the higher stages of life, embodying the initial awakening, the discipline, and the fruition on the higher plain." In all this "the principle of progress is from within."[2]

In other words, fundamentally education stimulates and assists certain natural, rhythmic cravings within the organism.[3] And apparently the satisfaction of such cravings results in "enjoyment," one of the fundamental springs of the educational process. "Now the natural mode by which living organisms are excited toward suitable self-development is enjoyment."[4] "Joy is the normal, healthy spur for the *élan vital* . . . we should seek to arrange the development of character along a path of activity, in itself pleasurable."[5] "Unless the pupils are continually sustained by the evocation of interest, the acquirement of technique, and the excitement of success, they can never make progress, and will certainly lose heart."[6]

Even for the seemingly more formidable part of Whitehead's program, his emphasis on abstract ideas, he relies on enjoyment and interest. So the older practical reason, concerned with the problem-solving of staying alive, is seen as stimulated by a "primitive deep-seated satisfaction arising out of an immemorial heredity."[7] The history of the speculative reason is much shorter, but it too is regarded as inherent—in Whitehead's figure, as "a tropism to the beckoning light."[8]

Enjoyment makes for interest, and without interest there can be no attention or apprehension.[9] To a certain extent the student can provide his own enjoyment by interesting himself in things which are worth doing and worth thinking about. "There is great satisfaction in doing things skillfully, and in understanding all about what you are doing, and in thinking of how it all bears on the lives of others around you."[10] This process of self-development can be aided from without,[11] and is encouraged by the proper environment.[12]

The obverse is also true. The student can be harmed by an unfavorable environment.

Whitehead realizes that students differ in native ability, in social class, in their prospects in life, in their backgrounds of experience, and all the rest. He realizes that the same level of achievement is not possible for all students and that interests do not all run in the same direction. He is careful, therefore, continually to remind us that his statements about education must refer mainly to rather vague groups, average students or students in general.[13]

Furthermore, though Whitehead considers that learning is a natural process, he does not conclude from this fact that it is an easy process or one which automatically takes place. Life, too, is a natural process, but the organism may find the struggle for existence hard or may fail in the attempt. Both these possibilities are true of learning also. There is no royal road to learning through an airy path of brilliant generalizations,[14] and no reform in education can abolish the necessity for hard work and exact knowledge.[15] There will undoubtedly be gray times of hard work through which only the student's grit will bring him.[16] Whitehead can hope only to reduce the difficulty, not remove it. Thus, in the stage of romance the student has little discipline and considerable freedom. If this stage is properly handled, it naturally brings on the following stage of precision.[17] The demands of the stage of precision are much more rigorous; but, if both stages are properly handled, the student should have developed certain habits, interests, and abilities which will stand him in good stead. They will, in fact, lead to the only discipline important for its own sake, self-discipline. He will "know how to go about his work, will want to make a good job of it, and can safely be trusted with the details."[18]

This mention of details in connection with enjoyment brings us back to a point we have already seen at length. Whitehead wishes to emphasize "leading principles" and "general ideas." The traditional subjects were educational because they did implant ideas, and hence "civilizing" new subjects involves transforming them into real vehicles for the inculcation of ideas.[19] But there is nothing harder to transmit to pupils than "real general ideas" as distinct from pretentious phrases or vague generalizations.[20] But since generalizations escape "inertness" by being based on and applied to details, "Interest depends on background, that is to say, upon the relations of the new element of thought or perception to the pre-existing mental furniture. If your children have not got the right background, even 'the survival of the fittest' will fail to enthuse them."[21]

By maintaining a proper balance between general ideas and the details relevant to them, Whitehead hopes to keep interest alive. But he admits that it is difficult to take a class very far along the road of precision without some dulling of interest.[22] This deadening effect is felt even in those areas where interest and motivation are strongest, specialized or technical study. In these areas Whitehead feels that education is fundamentally easier because the student is studying what he wants to know,[23] but the necessary training dulls the equally necessary imagination and initiative, despite the best efforts of the teacher.[24]

But, however interest is maintained (if it is maintained), there is something beyond interest. In fact, interest itself is impossible without ideals, "some hopes of the betterment of human society, some joy in making others happy, some courage in facing the obstacles to progress." But if such idealism is to be more than a "fluffy emotion," it must be based upon exact knowledge. Hence arises a quasi-paradox: No education without the interest which springs from idealism, but no solid idealism with education.[25] Only a constant interplay between the three makes the desired result possible.

One may well ask—and many have asked it of Whitehead's educational program—whether all students have such interests and ideals, or whether they can be led to seek to acquire them. Or the same general question may be restated in other terms which are also important for Whitehead: Do all students possess the desire to acquire a disinterested understanding of the universe? We have seen repeatedly his emphasis on the general ideas which produce "understanding." He believes that "there is a strong moral intuition that speculative understanding for its own sake is one of the elements of the good life." Yet he is equally quick to admit that not all men share this feeling. "Unlike some other moral feelings, this intuition is not widespread. Throughout the generality of mankind it flickers with very feeble intensity."[26] And the very possession of the speculative reason itself is apparently far from universally distributed. "But what distinguishes men from the animals, *some* humans from other humans, is the inclusion in their natures, waveringly and dimly, of a disturbing element."[27] Quite clearly, then, all men are not troubled by this disturbing element to the same degree, and, or so it would seem, all men are not equally motivated toward this quest for understanding.

To sum up our discussion thus far, Whitehead sees the student essentially as in the process of self-development. The purpose of education is to guide and foster this process. The data available to various people in concrescence—i.e., their hereditary and environmental factors—differ. The same paths of development are not equally open to all. Nor is the optimum self-development probably open to any one of them. The best that can be hoped for is that such powers for development as lie within the individual will exert their best potential as a result of the fostering of interest and enjoyment.

Fundamentally Whitehead tends to be optimistic. "Some measure of genius is the rightful inheritance of every man."[28] But on the other side of the ledger, Whitehead speaks of the dullness of the average student and notes that the intellectual curiosity of the speculative reason (on which he seems to depend so much) is a rather rare occurrence.[29] This attitude seems, to say the least, somewhat contradictory to the general optimistic tone of much of his educational writing. Perhaps Whitehead merely exhibits, however, that odd blend of optimism and pessimism which is often the hallmark of the experienced teacher. At bottom all teachers are optimistic; otherwise they would probably not remain in the profession. They continually hope to find students who will live up to their expectations. And, over the years, some students do—at least enough of them come close enough to keep up the teacher's hopes. But even the most optimistic, complacent, or unperceptive teacher eventually comes to realize that most students fall short—not of the teacher's goals—but of the student's own potentialities and aspirations. Some teachers eventually come to feel that the ultimate limit of the student's development is the student's own responsibility. But others agree with Whitehead that the organism is not the *sole* criterion of its own development. The organism must have some sense of worth beyond itself.[30] This striving against the limits of actuality and even of possibility is that adventure which produces the creative advance. If Whitehead often seems unduly optimistic, if he seems to attribute to the average student the same curiosity, diligence, and capacity which were his to an unusual degree, perhaps he is merely hoping to keep both learning and teaching from falling into a dull routine.

To turn to the role of the teacher, the essential elements are clear from what has already been said. Since the student is engaged in a natural process of self-development, the function of the teacher is to aid and guide this process.

> The teacher has a double function. It is for him to elicit enthusiasm by resonance from his own personality, and to create the environment of a larger knowledge and a firmer purpose. He is there to avoid the waste which in the lower stages of existence is nature's way of evolution.[31]

This statement sums up the major elements in Whitehead's view of the teacher's function and also incorporates some of the problems inherent in a view of this kind.

The importance of enthusiasm on the part of the teacher is obvious from points already made in regard to the student. Since there can be no development in the student without interest and since the source of interest is enjoyment,[32] "the first thing that a teacher has to do when he enters the classroom is to make his class glad to be there."[33] In part he achieves this by himself being "alive with living thoughts."[34] And in this connection the most important characteristic of the teacher is imagination.[35] Whitehead most frequently speaks of the negative side of this matter. Without imagination, learning becomes stale (like yesterday's fish) and the possibility of novelty is lost. "Schemes of orthodoxies" are the result unless knowledge is "lighted up with imagination."[36] The old patterns, the old perspectives, will persist unless imagination offers new ones which make novelty possible.

Imagination is, therefore, an important element in the genius of the teacher. Another element is involved in that avoidance of waste mentioned in the quotation with which we began this section. In accordance with the principle of rhythm, the teacher should make his efforts at stimulation correspond to the natural rhythmic cravings of the pupil.[37] At the stage of romance this effort is fairly easy. Exploration and browsing are likely to be interesting and enjoyable because interest and enjoyment tend to be the chief principles which direct them. But once this stage has passed, the problem becomes more difficult. Many things have been found out, and though the student may have established good habits and may have a natural craving for precision once romance is over, "the responsibility of the teacher is immense. To speak the truth,

except in the rare case of genius in the teacher, I do
not think it is possible to take a whole class very far
along the road of precision without some dulling of the
interest."[38]  It is the teacher's genius which allows
him to select the proper materials and procedures.[39]
As we have already seen in detail, this task of selection is a point to which Whitehead continually gives
primary emphasis. It is not enough that the curriculum be pruned of irrelevant stuff of inferior importance so that major ideas and their relevant details
will stand out.[40]

> After all the child is the heir to long ages of civilization
> and it is absurd to let him wander in the intellectual maze
> of men in the Glacial Epoch.  Accordingly a certain point-
> ing out of facts, and of simplifying ideas and of usual
> names, really strengthens the natural impetus of the
> pupil.[41]

All this is summed up in the dictum, "A certain ruthless definiteness is essential in education."[42]  Moreover,
"the environment within which the mind is working
must be carefully selected. It must, of course, be
chosen to suit the child's stage of growth, and must
be adapted to individual needs."[43]  Since all this
depends on the genius of the teacher, it is not supris-
ing that

> we are discovering that in schools you cannot do without
> genius, genius of character, genius of insight, and genius
> of intellectual enthusiasm.  Authorities who want suc-
> cessful schools must see to it that the conditions in the
> teaching profession are those in which genius can thrive.[44]

Despite this emphasis on the importance of the teacher, however, education remains for Whitehead a *natural* process of self-development. Though the unskilled practitioner can damage the delicate organism, professors and teachers tend to forget that they are "only subordinate elements in the education of a grown man, and that, in their own good time our pupils will learn for themselves."[45] Thus Whitehead's position on education, especially as it concerns the role of the teacher, is similar to that of Aristotle and Aquinas.

> It must never be forgotten that education is not a process of packing articles in a trunk. . . . It is, of course, a process completely of its own peculiar genus. Its nearest analogue is the assimilation of food by a living organism. . . . In a sense it is imposition from without; but in a deeper sense it answers to the call of life within the child.[46]

This position, as usual, involves a number of familiar questions concerning the limits within which the teacher may properly operate—or to put the matter more bluntly, the extent to which the teacher is entitled to intervene actively in the pupil's process of self-development. Such right as the teacher has seems to rest on that "larger knowledge" and "surer purpose" already mentioned.[47] But insofar as both these are limited, the right too is limited. Unfortunately Whitehead does not go into details on this and other major points. He does say:

> We are only just realizing that the art and science of education require a genius and a study of their own; and

that this genius and this science are more than a bare
knowledge of some branch of science or literature.[48]

But how this genius and science are developed or what
their contents are, he does not specify.
As a consequence he has little to say about the problems of teacher training or teacher improvement. To
be sure, he does suggest that the way to make the
teachers acquire the important characteristic of "imagination" is to encourage them to research.[49] But
beyond that, he seems to rely on the natural genius of
the teacher, given maximum scope within his institution. This view of the matter naturally encounters
some difficulties in situations where the number of
teachers needed is greater than the number of natural
pedagogical geniuses, as Whitehead would probably
agree.

Education inevitably goes on in a context or milieu,
stretching from the student's family and his immediate community, through his culture with its institutions, mores, and organization into a political state,
out to the world as a whole. All these factors shape
education and are, in their turn, partly altered by it.

Whitehead offers relatively little explicit comment
on the relation of the educational process to these
factors. To be sure, he frequently refers to the influence of geographical, social, and political phenomena
on education,[50] and, conversely, to the effects which
education has or can have upon social and political
affairs.[51] But the total bulk of these comments is not
large, and many of them are little more than obiter
dicta.

This lack of explicit treatment of these important

matters seems to arise from two chief causes. One lies in the formal structure of Whitehead's educational and cosmological doctrines. Since, for Whitehead, education is self-development, education and what it means in understanding and power to the person who possesses it are to be seen in the perspective of that individual, just as in the cosmological doctrine the universe comes to a focus on the entity which is in the process of self-creation. But self-development does not take place in a vacuum any more than does the self-creation of the actual entity. We must not conceive the mentality of men as their private act of internal self-development. This private aspect of culture has been stressed far too strongly.[52] The mutual immanence of things makes it certain that any activity or being will necessarily involve the rest of the cosmos. This statement is as true of education as it is of the concrescence of the actual entity. Whitehead would not, therefore, wish to deny or ignore the existence of social, political, or other forces which bear on education. But because his system centers on the individual, these other matters merge with the other "data" which the universe offers. They are, therefore, talked about by indirection, so to speak, in that to talk about self-development or self-creation is in fact to talk about the entire universe.

But in Whitehead's system there is a second cause for his comparative neglect of these matters, and this cause is constitutive, not formal, in his doctrine. The individual is the locus of value, the center where values are found. As we saw earlier, the fundamental instance of value in the universe is the act of self-realization by an entity. To be is to be valuable. And

Whitehead's educational and cosmological doctrines rest to a considerable degree on the primacy in his system of the unique individual.

His comment on aesthetic enjoyment can probably be taken as typical of his attitude on most topics:

> Apart from large uniformities, all effort is ineffective. But all intensity of enjoyment, sustained with the strength of individual character, arises from individual taste diversifying the stream of uniformity. Destroy individuality, and you are left with a vacancy of aesthetic feeling. . . . [53]

As a result, he states the general relation between the individual and his society quite bluntly:

> The worth of any social system depends on the value experience it promotes among individual human beings. . . . A community life is a mode of eliciting value for the people concerned. . . Any particular community life touches only part of the nature of each civilized man. If the man be wholly subordinated to the common life, he is dwarfed.[54]

This point of view is deep and pervasive in Whitehead.[55] We see this same attitude from another perspective if we remember that it is the essence of education to be "religious"[56] and that for Whitehead "religion is what the individual does with his own solitariness."[57] Probably, then, his comments in connection with religion apply to education as well:

> You cannot abstract society from man; most psychology is herd-psychology. But all collective emotions leave untouched the awful ultimate fact, which is the human being, consciously alone with itself, for its own sake.[58]

In short, Whitehead is not the man to see education primarily as the instrument of the state to improve its citizens or the tool of society in achieving social cohesiveness. Education can and does serve those purposes. But it should not become subservient to them. Education must remain for Whitehead a process of self-development, the individual's opportunity to make the most of what he has both in and around him.

1. *Essays in Science and Philosophy*, p. 128; *The Aims of Education*, p. 61.

2. *The Aims of Education*, p. 62.

3. *Ibid.*, pp. 43, 31.

4. *Ibid.*, p. 48.

5. *Ibid.*, p. 49.

6. *Ibid.*, p. 60.

7. *The Function of Reason*, p. 13.

8. *Ibid.*, p. 51.

9. *The Aims of Education*, p. 48. Enjoyment is no less important in work than in education. For invention and for the development of the new ideas, both workmen and employers must enjoy their work (*ibid.*, p. 68).

10. *Essays in Science and Philosophy*, p. 128. Cf. also *The Aims of Education*, p. 74; "The pleasure which art and science can give to toil is the enjoyment which arises from successfully directed attention."

11. *The Aims of Education*, p. 61.

12. *Ibid.*, p. 51.

13. *Ibid.*, pp. 7–8, 11, 14–15, 36, 39, 43, 51, 63, 85, 95, 96–97, 100, 103, 119, 122, 123, 132; *Essays in Science and Philosophy*, pp. 9, 130, 134–35.

14. *The Aims of Education*, p. 10.

15. *Essays in Science and Philosophy*, p. 143.

16. *Ibid.*, p. 128.

17. *The Aims of Education*, p. 52.

18. *Ibid.*, p. 55.

19. *Ibid.*, p. 96; *Essays in Science and Philosophy*, p. 130.

20. *Essays in Science and Philosophy*, p. 131.

21. *Ibid.*, p. 142.

22. *The Aims of Education*, pp. 55–56.

23. *Ibid.*, pp. 17–18.

24. *Ibid.*, p. 144.

25. *Essays in Science and Philosophy*, p. 128.

26. *The Function of Reason*, p. 30.

27. *Ibid.*, p. 51 (italics added).

28. *Essays in Science and Philosophy*, p. 145.

29. *The Function of Reason*, p. 30.

30. *Modes of Thought*, p. 140.

31. *The Aims of Education*, p. 62.

32. *Ibid.*, pp. 48–49.

33. *Essays in Science and Philosophy*, p. 127.

34. *The Aims of Education*, p. v.

35. *Ibid.*, pp. 135–52 *passim*, especially 147.

36. *Essays in Science and Philosophy*, pp. 23–24.

37. *The Aims of Education*, pp. 30–31.

38. *Ibid.*, pp. 55–56.

39. *Ibid.*, pp. 7–8.

40. *Ibid.*, pp. 56, 119.

41. *Ibid.*, pp. 51–52.

42. *Ibid.*, p. 57.

43. *Ibid.*, p. 51.

44. *Essays in Science and Philosophy*, p. 127.

45. *The Aims of Education*, p. 53.

46. *Ibid.*, p. 51.

47. *Ibid.*, p. 62.

48. *Ibid.*, p. 6.

49. *Ibid.*, p. 146.

50. For example, *Essays in Science and Philosophy*, pp. 9–10, 27, 29–30, 164.

51. For example, *The Aims of Education*, pp. 64–65, 68, 70, 84, 90, 137, 143, 148; *Essays in Science and Philosophy*, pp. 14, 124–26.

52. *Essays in Science and Philosophy*, p. 148.

53. *Ibid.*, p. 118.

54. *Ibid.*, p. 52.

55. So, for example, emphasis on "isolation" marked his political views prior to World War II (*ibid.*, pp. 44 ff.).

56. *The Aims of Education*, p. 23.

57. *Religion in the Making*, p. 16.

58. *Ibid.*, p. 16.

# XIII. Whiteheadian Cosmology and Whiteheadian Education

AT THIS POINT we are in a position to turn back to the list of "expectations for education" formulated in Chapter VIII on the basis of Whitehead's cosmology. We can now determine the extent to which Whitehead's educational position as he actually states it appears consonant with them. The arabic numbers in the following discussion correspond to those of the propositions listed earlier.

1. Education does indeed seem for Whitehead to be a process of self-development analogous in some respects to the concrescence of an actual entity. This resemblance is, of course, very general, but its significance becomes more evident and more important in conjunction with the next five, less general, propositions listed as expectations. Nonetheless, if we inquire into why he sees learning as rhythmic or why novelty, imagination, and suggestiveness are important in education, we find many parts of Whitehead's theory offering what seems more than coincidental likeness: the rhythmic nature of life, growth, and creativity,

concrescence as the prehension of data which include as yet unrealized possibilities and the like.

2. Whitehead's educational views do appear to rest quite obviously on the belief that, like concrescence, education is a natural process for which the student has a natural inclination and even a natural craving. Whitehead is sometimes accused of "intellectualism" because he assumes that students generally have a drive toward learning, particularly toward learning in the sense of a theoretical understanding of the world. He does not stress extrinsic motivations and rewards, or even the stimulus of immediate practical or personal problems. His various curriculums clearly imply that all students have some capacity for the development of the speculative reason, or, at least, that they should have some opportunity for the development of such capacity as they have.

Whitehead's position is sometimes explained as due to his generalizing his personal intellectual interests to mankind at large or to his experience's being limited to the British secondary school and university of his day, with their student bodies very strictly selected on the basis of intellectual interest and competence. Both these facts may well be involved. It is worth noting, however, that Whitehead's cosmological view would, of itself, lead him to much this same position. A favorable environment, especially one rich in those ideas and suggestions which mark the advance of civilization, would do much to encourage an interest in speculative understanding. Whitehead naturally sees the educational situation as one in which to maximize such capacity as exists.

3. As we have seen in detail in Whitehead's comment about the role of the teacher, he regards the function of formal education as that of merely facilitating this natural process. Education can no more be done for the student than concrescence can be done for an entity. Hence Whitehead warns that teachers easily come to regard their role as more important than it actually is. Formal education can reduce the waste which marks all natural processes, can offer a favorable environment, can be suggestive, and can prevent ideas from becoming inert. But the operative element is always the student and his internal urge toward development.

4. Student responsibility actually receives somewhat less emphasis than might be expected from the cosmological doctrine alone. This situation may perhaps be adequately accounted for by several facts. First, Whitehead is writing from the background of the British tradition in which the student at the levels of secondary and higher education has considerably more freedom and responsibility than the equivalent American student. Thus the point may be too obvious for Whitehead to bother to comment on it or so indigenous in his educational situation that Whitehead is not even aware of it. A second possible explanation is that most of Whitehead's educational writings were originally lectures addressed to groups of teachers. He thus naturally stresses the functions and duties of teachers rather than the role of the student. The point is, however, clearly implicit in his general position, as is most apparent in the ancillary function which he assigns to the teacher and the educational institution.

5. The educational writings do stress the development of the unique individual. Though Whitehead does see certain general characteristics and qualities as desirable in all educated people and though he offers specific curriculums rather than programs developed by free election, he leaves wide scope for individual variation and development. His continual emphasis on the importance of specialization (with its inevitable individualization) is alone almost enough to prove the point. If we add his abhorrence of academic orthodoxy and dogma and his emphasis on suggestiveness and "learning lighted up with imagination," we see that education as a voyage into the unknown is not seeking to produce social, intellectual, economic, or any other kind of conformity, but rather "depth of individuality."

6. The function of education as that of furnishing ideas and ideals is one of the most striking features of Whitehead's pedagogical writings. The stress on sensitivity, suggestiveness, novelty, imagination, and the rest is so repeated and obvious as to require no further comment here.

7. In view of the importance of good patterning in Whitehead's cosmological system it receives surprisingly little explicit emphasis in his educational writings. Not that it is ignored. Seeing the task of the university as the achievement of a harmony of diverse things, the important place given to art, and the prolonged study of literary models and historical example are all instances of its explicit mention and implicit involvement.

8. Ideas and ideals must not be merely seen and entertained; they must be made real. Certainly Whitehead's educational program makes full provision for this practical and operative effort. "Specialized knowledge," "power," "duty," "effectiveness," "style," "utilization," and "professionalized knowledge" are all topics we have seen treated at great length in Whitehead's programs, and they all bear on this issue. As was to be expected, the student is being prepared to live in no dream world; he is to make the dreams reality.

9. The expectation that both the speculative and practical functions of reason would be emphasized is more than fully substantiated. As we have seen, Whitehead's curriculums are all built around the fusion of the understanding of the speculative reason, on the one hand, with the power and effectiveness of the practical reason, on the other.

10. Educated persons and educational programs are all clearly taken as instances of patterning and judged as such. In regard to both, Whitehead sees the desirable as the interweaving of very diverse strands, and the excellence of the product lies in the totality achieved. Thus in the person the qualities of the amateur are to be joined with those of the specialist, vocational education is to be interwoven with liberal education. But the end is an organic whole, the educated man with the seamless cloak of learning undivided.

To a striking extent, then, Whitehead's position on education is in many respects what we should have expected from an examination of his general philosophic position. He could, of course, have arrived at a similar educational position from rather different philosophic grounds. And certainly much of the detail of his plans stems from the general kind of education with which he and his audiences were familiar. But when due allowance has been made for both these facts, the correspondence between Whitehead's philosophic doctrine and his educational views appears both extensive and fundamental.

We need not imply that such points as the rhythmic nature of learning or the importance of suggestiveness and understanding are logically deduced from his metaphysical principles to see that there is a marked degree of congruence. And this accord is sufficient for many educational purposes. We need not hold that the relation between the two parts of Whitehead's doctrine is as close as those of, say, Herbart and Froebel, each of whom went to great pains to make his philosophic and educational systems interlock. We can, at the other extreme, assert that the situation here is not that of Kant, whose "Lecture Notes on Pedagogy" show no trace of the author of the three great Critiques, or that of Locke, whose *Some Thoughts Concerning Education* is almost equally innocent of traces of the *Essay Concerning Human Understanding*. It is sufficient that Whitehead fell toward the middle, and closer to Herbart and Froebel, for us to be able to use, with due caution and with adequate recognition of the problems involved in analyzing the precise relation, his cosmological works as supplement to his educational writings.

# XIV.  Whitehead as a Philosopher for Education

MUCH OF Whitehead's contribution as a philosopher of education lies, of course, in the general principles and specific comments cited in the preceding chapters. But Whitehead offers more than that.

We saw earlier that there are two important functions which educators often hope that an educational philosophy will perform for them. One is to provide a comprehensive matrix within which educational problems, with their multiple aspects and their varied but partial scientific answers, could be examined and treated with some degree of completeness and consistency. The second is to offer some means of dealing with the problem of value. Whitehead's doctrine performs both these tasks.

Whitehead's system does indeed offer a comprehensive matrix. Within a system which sweeps from general principles like creativity to the particular concrescences of given actual entities, everything can find a place; and not merely a place but a place which relates that item to the rest of the system. This fact is most importantly true of Whitehead's more specifically educational principles such as the rhythmic bases of learning, the importance of understanding, and the uniqueness of the individual. These are not mere isolated dicta or fugitive insights. They are built-in parts of a comprehensive system and can be interpreted and applied as parts of that system. Thus, given a case, a problem, or a situation, the educator does find in Whitehead's work a context within which to fit the question and to see it in its relations.

To be sure, Whitehead's system is not so rigid and mechanical that it can serve as a sort of automatic computer. The educator cannot merely drop questions into it and wait for the answers to emerge of themselves. Philosophic systems are instruments to aid thinking. They cannot serve as substitutes for it. They suggest matters of which some account must be taken and offer an orderly procedure for taking such account.

From the very nature of Whitehead's system, educators may encounter one kind of difficulty fairly frequently, what may be called a lack of "middle principles." Quite properly for Whitehead's own purposes, he tends to work in his cosmology either at the level of abstract cosmic generalizations (like creativity) or at the highly specific level of the self-creation of a single actual entity. His educational writings likewise tend to emphasize either very general principles or quite specific examples of their application. The educator may sometimes wish for "more in between," for subordinate principles which will lead precisely from the general principle to the specific decision or case.

For example, Whitehead, as we have seen, lays great stress on application. Only through application are ideas kept from becoming inert and only through it are both learning about the world and the remaking of it possible. But particular educational problems and programs may raise major questions about the precise kind and amount of application specifically desirable; and these questions may not be clearly settled by Whitehead's general principle of application, even in conjunction with his other major principles.

Whitehead himself, however, seemed to anticipate little difficulty in this regard. In his educational lectures he frequently mentions the greater practical experience of the schoolmen who constituted his audience and implies that they will have no difficulty in working out more detailed solutions along the general lines he has sketched. Quite possibly the final judgment on this point must be empirical. As Whitehead's thought becomes more accessible and as more educators attempt to apply it to a wide range of problems and situations, the ease or difficulty of its utilization will become apparent.

One cannot ask, of course, that an educational philosopher chart everything. Whitehead has reared an enormous structure and given a spacious framework to guide educational thought and practice. The immediate need is the increased utilization of it in a wide variety of situations.

The second great area in which philosophy is expected to make a contribution is in regard to the problem of value. As we have seen, Whitehead has an aesthetic theory of value, one which involves the judgment of good patterning. Whitehead is quick to point out that we know too little about patterns of all sorts for him to be able to give detailed criteria. Such detailed studies of patterning as those available in symbolic logic and aesthetics are far too limited in scope to be more than suggestive. Much more work will have to be done before "importance" and its sub-species in morality and the rest can be competently judged.

In this area, then, we must recognize that White-head is far from presenting an adequate and simple answer, as he would be the first to assert. But no one else can do it either. Whitehead's merit lies in that he at least poses the problem in the right way and suggests the kind of standard which will solve it, even though he cannot offer a final solution or exact criteria. Certainly the educator will receive some help in making his own standards if he realizes the proper bases of his own judgments. He is not looking for particular elements or items which will, in themselves, constitute the desirable. Rather, he is looking for that best ordering of the elements constituting the given situation. The general criteria of unity, balance, and the rest will give the general standards, but the question of how well they are embodied in individual nexūs and societies is a matter of particular judgment.

But Whitehead's greatest contribution to modern education possibly lies in the number of points at which he can serve as a needed corrective to certain tendencies in current American education and in contemporary American society.

The first of these is his emphasis upon understanding. It has become a commonplace to point out that America is generally weak in pure theory and pure research. Our ethos seems to find technology and applied science more congenial. We love to solve technical or practical problems or to produce things. Our

educational programs and objectives are often dominated by vocational aims. All these are the concern of
the practical reason. Whitehead does not deny their
importance. But his emphasis on the speculative reason, which seeks to understand experience for the
sheer joy of knowing, can serve as a desirable supplement and counterweight to our usual habits and
practice.

A second point of this kind is his emphasis on wisdom as the way in which knowledge is held. His moral
is not new. But the point merits continual restatement
because students, teachers, and society as a whole
easily come to feel that knowledge alone is enough.
The reminder that knowledge is necessary but not
sufficient for the development of the individual and
the advance of civilization is, consequently, always
in order.

A third valuable point is his emphasis on the individual. Again, it is a commonplace to say that we
live in the age of Organization Man. However desirable
"togetherness," "groupiness," and "other-directedness"
may be within limits, our present society tends to
overdo them. Without falling in a position of extreme
individualism, Whitehead attempts to redress the balance by stressing the individual as the locus of value
and by subordinating social and political organizations
to him.

The fourth point is something of a corollary to the
preceding. The individual is responsible; to some degree he is the master of his fate. In an age when
individual responsibility is too frequently shrugged
off by blaming "an unfortunate environment," "the
pressure of circumstances," "poor inheritance," "the

system," or some other external and allegedly uncontrollable force, Whitehead stresses existence as self-creation. Without seeking to deny matters of brute fact or the reality of impoverished or unfavorable environments, Whitehead suggests the extent to which the organism can minimize these adverse influences, and he indicates some of the means through selection and patterning by which the organism can achieve this end.

Fifth, Whitehead's doctrine is spacious. He does not arbitrarily exclude vast stretches of human experience from consideration on some dogmatic ground. As one interested in science, he tries to give science its full due. He sees science and mathematics as the great means for understanding the world, and his suggested curriculums have a heavy weighting of science. On the other hand, his views are not restricted to science. He has the haunting fear that much of life may slip through the meshes of the scientific net and that the world may vanish into differential equations. For the treatment of some potential subject matters found in human experience, scientific procedures may not be merely as yet imperfect, but actually imperfectible. Hence he makes a real place for other modes of dealing with experience. Thus art, for example, is more than an honorific, leisure-time activity, for its principles underlie reality and value in the universe. Experience with art and the study of art (in Whitehead's broad sense of that term) thus tell us something about experience in their own way. Similarly, religious experience (as distinct from religious dogma) is something more than outworn superstition. Despite the errors and biases which have marked the history

of human religious experience, Whitehead believes that
if these insights are properly handled, religious experience, too, can be a source of information about the
cosmos and man's experience in it. Educators who
feel that many modern views have defined the area of
rational thought too narrowly will welcome Whitehead's broader scope.

Sixth, Whitehead's system is open at the edges and
flexible at the core. Like most first-rate philosophers,
he attempts to interest us in a quest, not a cure. He
does not believe that the human race has exhausted all
the varieties of experience. He doubts that we yet
have an adequate approximation to the language and
other conceptual tools which would enable us to analyze
and understand experience adequately. And within
his system, Whitehead is equally modest and tentative.
As we have seen, he offers his set of fundamental cosmological terms as merely a first approximation in the
certainty that they will necessarily be revised as our
experience and our insight progress. During his life-
time he was quite ready to admit that some major
elements in his doctrine probably needed to be recast.
But in this connection it is instructive to apply to
Whitehead himself his own comment about Plato:

> He is never entirely self-consistent, and rarely explicit
> and devoid of ambiguity. He feels the difficulties and ex-
> presses his perplexities. No one could be perplexed over
> Aristotle's classifications; whereas Plato moves about amid
> a fragmentary system like a man dazed by his own pene-
> tration.[1]

If this estimate of Plato is sound, we do well to remember that Plato, despite these shortcomings, has en-

lightened and enlivened philosophic and educational thought for several millenia. Even if similar charges can be brought against Whitehead (as they have been), his doctrine may be no less stimulating to educational thought and action.

The final point may seem to share the fallaciousness of the argument *ad hominem*, though perhaps this argument is less invalid in education, in morals, and in similar fields than it is elsewhere. The character of the man himself urges no small claim for his thought. That here is a great person is the impression thrust upon the reader of Whitehead's work at nearly every page. One can hardly fail to be struck by the urbanity, insight, sensitivity, wisdom, and moral earnestness of the man. Any time and place has too few of such men, and only a minute percentage of them are ever directly concerned with education. To view the world and education from the perspective of such a man cannot fail to benefit us.

1. *Adventures of Ideas*, pp. 187–88.

# Index

Abstract, the, 18–19, 64, 105, 117, 126

Actual entity, 31–34, 36, 38, 39, 40, 42, 45, 49, 52, 53, 62, 85, 87, 99–100, 160, 165, 171, 172; *see also* Occasion of experience

Adventure, 40, 66, 96, 97, 103, 126, 155

Aesthetic, the, 44–45, 63–64, 79, 87, 125, 126, 161, 173–74; *see also* Art

Aims of education, 91–106, 134–35, 137, 142, 146, 175

Amateur, the, 91, 93, 169; *see also* General education; Liberal education

Application of learning, 98–99, 106, 111–12, 117, 132, 138, 139, 140, 141, 142, 172–73

Aristotle, 98

Art, 41, 50, 64, 66, 71, 73, 94, 97, 102, 113, 124–26, 134, 136, 144, 168, 176; *see also* Aesthetic

Beauty, 66, 74, 83, 92, 93, 100, 126, 142, 144

Burns, H. W., 10–11

Cambridge University, 5

Chicago, University of, 13

Chronology of Whitehead's writings, 5–6, 10, 84

Civilization, definition of, 65–66, 97, 101, 126

Consciousness, 42, 51, 52, 72, 75, 77, 149

Concrescence, 14, 34–37, 42, 51, 62, 65, 66, 72, 75, 77, 78, 85, 86, 95, 154, 160, 165, 166, 167, 171

Concrete, the, 24, 64, 72, 105, 114, 117, 126

Co-ordination of studies, 140–41

Cosmology, 5, 6, 9, 10, 12, 23–29, 83–84, 96, 102–3, 142, 160, 165–70, 172, 177; *see also* Metaphysics; Philosophy

Creativity, 37, 42, 45–46, 49, 70, 85, 86, 165, 171, 172

Curriculum, 88–89, 104, 106, 107–9, 119, 121–47, 168; literary, 106, 122–24, 133–36; mathematical-scientific, 106, 119, 136–40; technical, 106, 144; *see also* Application; Art; Co-ordination of studies; Detail; Expert, the; General education; Generalization, stage of; History; Idea; Knowledge; Language; Liberal education; Literature; Logic; Mathematics; Music; Religion; Rhythm; Romance; Science; Sequence; Specialization; Specialized knowledge;